PostgreSQL 9 Administration Cookbook: LITE

Configuration, Monitoring and Maintenance

Simon Riggs

Hannu Krosing

BIRMINGHAM - MUMBAI

PostgreSQL 9 Administration Cookbook: LITE

First published: April 2011

Production Reference: 1130411

Published by Packt Publishing Ltd.
32 Lincoln Road
Olton
Birmingham, B27 6PA, UK.

ISBN 978-1-849516-42-6

www.packtpub.com

Cover Image by John M. Quick (john.m.quick@gmail.com)

Credits

Authors

Simon Riggs

Hannu Krosing

Reviewers

Gabriele Bartolini

Dimitri Fontaine

Acquisition Editor

Sarah Cullington

Technical Editor

Prashant Macha

Indexer

Hemangini Bari

Production Coordinator

Adline Swetha Jesuthas

Cover Work

Kruthika Bangera

About the Authors

Simon Riggs is a major developer and one of the few committers on the PostgreSQL database project, as well as CTO of 2ndQuadrant, providing 24x7 support and services to PostgreSQL users worldwide.

Simon works actively as a database architect and support troubleshooter, skills which drive and shape his contributions to the development of operational features for PostgreSQL. Feature credits include Point in Time Recovery, Warm Standby replication, Hot Standby, Asynchronous Commit, Partitioning and many other performance and tuning features. His designs and solutions can be found throughout the PostgreSQL code and documentation.

Simon has also previously worked with Oracle, Teradata, and DB2 and holds multiple certifications. His previous experience covers management and senior technical roles in the banking, telecommunications and software industries. Simon's early research work has been published by the Royal Society.

Hannu Krosing is a principal consultant at 2ndQuadrant and a Technical Advisor at Ambient Sound Investments. As the original database architect at Skype Technologies, Hannu was responsible for designing the Skytools suite of replication and scalability technologies. Hannu has more than 12 years experience working with and contributing to the PostgreSQL project.

About the Reviewers

Gabriele Bartolini is a long time open-source programmer, writing Linux/Unix applications in C and C++ for over 10 years, specializing in search engines and web analytics with large databases.

Gabriele has a degree in Statistics from the University of Florence. His areas of expertise are data mining and data warehousing, having worked on web traffic analysis in Australia and Italy.

Gabriele is a consultant with 2ndQuadrant and an active member of the international PostgreSQL community.

Gabriele currently lives in Prato, a small but vibrant city located in the northern part of Tuscany, Italy. His second home is Melbourne, Australia, where he has studied at Monash University and worked in the ICT sector.

His hobbies include "calcio" (football or soccer, depending on which part of the world you come from) and playing his Fender Stratocaster electric guitar.

> Thanks to my family, in particular Cathy who encourages me by saying there is always something new to learn.

Dimitri Fontaine is part of the PostgreSQL community and has been contributing to open source for more than 10 years. He is the lead developer of enterprise ready solutions such as pgloader (ETL), PostgreSQL prefix indexing (telephony routing), pg_staging (development environment maintenance from production backups), preprepare (allow easy usage of prepare statements behind a connection pooler), and some backports of recent PostgreSQL features

He also contributed to Skytools and the Londiste replication system and, authored a PHP layer for the PGQ event handler, allowing for robust asynchronous processing and code reuse.

Dimitri's passion is system architecture & design, with the goals of reduced maintenance time and very high availability

Professional experience, community involvement, and PostgreSQL expertise have led Dimitri to now work as a principal consultant at 2ndQuadrant, France.

Table of Contents

Preface

PostgreSQL is an advanced SQL database server, available on a wide range of platforms and is fast becoming one of the world's most popular server databases with an enviable reputation for performance, stability, and an enormous range of advanced features. PostgreSQL is one of the oldest open source projects, completely free to use, and developed by a very diverse worldwide community. Most of all, it just works!

One of the clearest benefits of PostgreSQL is that it is open source, meaning that you have a very permissive license to install, use, and distribute PostgreSQL without paying anyone any fees or royalties. On top of that, PostgreSQL is well-known as a database that stays up for long periods, and requires little or no maintenance in many cases. Overall, PostgreSQL provides a very low total cost of ownership.

PostgreSQL Administration Cookbook offers the information you need to manage your live production databases on PostgreSQL. The book contains insights direct from the main author of the PostgreSQL replication and recovery features, and the database architect of the most successful startup using PostgreSQL, Skype. This hands-on guide will assist developers working on live databases, supporting web or enterprise software applications using Java, Python, Ruby, .Net from any development framework. It's easy to manage your database when you've got PostgreSQL 9 Administration Cookbook at hand.

This practical guide gives you quick answers to common questions and problems, building on the authors' experience as trainers, users, and core developers of the PostgreSQL database server.

Each technical aspect is broken down into short recipes that demonstrate solutions with working code, and then explains why and how that works. The book is intended to be a desk reference for both new users and technical experts.

This book is a LITE edition of a longer book, PostgreSQL 9 Administration Cookbook. With the full edition, you get over 80 recipes on all the topics you need to for running an efficient PostgreSQL 9.0 database. In this edition, we'll look at three areas: configuration, monitoring and diagnosis, and setting up regular maintenance.

To find out more about upgrading to the full edition, visit www.packtpub. com/liteupgrade and log into your account for offers and help. If you don't have an account on PacktPub.com, visit today and set one up!

What this book covers

Chapter 1, Configuration, covers topics such as reading the fine manual (RTFM), planning a new database, changing parameters in your programs, the current configuration settings, parameters that are at non-default settings, updating the parameter file, setting parameters for particular groups of users, basic server configuration checklist, adding an external module into the PostgreSQL server, and running the server in power saving mode.

Chapter 2, Monitoring and Diagnosis, provides recipes that answer questions such as is the user connected?, what are they running?, are they active or blocked?, who is blocking them?, is anybody using a specific table?, when did anybody last use it?, how much disk space is used by temporary data?, and why are my queries slowing down? It also helps you in investigating and reporting a bug, producing a daily summary report of logfile errors, killing a specific session, and resolving an in-doubt prepared transaction.

Chapter 3, Regular Maintenance, provides useful recipes on controlling automatic database maintenance, avoiding auto freezing and page corruptions, avoiding transaction wraparound, removing old prepared transactions, actions for heavy users of temporary tables, identifying and fixing bloated tables and indexes, maintaining indexes, finding unused indexes, carefully removing unwanted indexes, and planning maintenance.

What you need for this book

We need the following software for this book:

- PostgreSQL 9.0 Server Software
- psql client utility (part of 9.0)
- pgAdmin3 1.12

Who this book is for

This book is for system administrators, database administrators, architects, developers, and anyone with an interest in planning for or running live production databases. This book is most suited to those who have some technical experience.

Conventions

In this book, you will find a number of styles of text that distinguish between different kinds of information. Here are some examples of these styles, and an explanation of their meaning.

Code words in text are shown as follows: "In PostgreSQL 9.0, the utility `pg_standby` is no longer required, as many of its features are now performed directly by the server."

A block of code is set as follows:

```
CREATE USER repuser
        SUPERUSER
        LOGIN
        CONNECTION LIMIT 1
        ENCRYPTED PASSWORD 'changeme';
```

When we wish to draw your attention to a particular part of a code block, the relevant lines or items are set in bold:

```
SELECT *
FROM mytable
WHERE   (col1, col2, … ,colN) IN
(SELECT col1, col2, … ,colN
   FROM mytable
   GROUP BY        col1, col2, … ,colN
   HAVING count(*) > 1);
```

Any command-line input or output is written as follows:

```
$ postgres --single -D /full/path/to/datadir postgres
```

New terms and important words are shown in bold. Words that you see on the screen, in menus or dialog boxes for example, appear in the text like this: " The Query tool has a good looking visual explain feature as well as a Graphical Query Builder, as shown in the following screenshot".

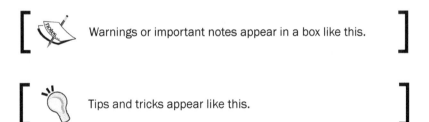

Warnings or important notes appear in a box like this.

Tips and tricks appear like this.

Reader feedback

Feedback from our readers is always welcome. Let us know what you think about this book—what you liked or may have disliked. Reader feedback is important for us to develop titles that you really get the most out of.

To send us general feedback, simply send an e-mail to feedback@packtpub.com, and mention the book title via the subject of your message.

If there is a book that you need and would like to see us publish, please send us a note in the SUGGEST A TITLE form on www.packtpub.com or e-mail suggest@packtpub.com.

If there is a topic that you have expertise in and you are interested in either writing or contributing to a book, see our author guide on www.packtpub.com/authors..

Customer support

Now that you are the proud owner of a Packt book, we have a number of things to help you to get the most from your purchase.

Downloading the example code for this book

You can download the example code files for all Packt books you have purchased from your account at http://www.PacktPub.com. If you purchased this book elsewhere, you can visit http://www.PacktPub.com/support and register to have the files e-mailed directly to you

Errata

Although we have taken every care to ensure the accuracy of our content, mistakes do happen. If you find a mistake in one of our books—maybe a mistake in the text or the code—we would be grateful if you would report this to us. By doing so, you can save other readers from frustration and help us improve subsequent versions of this book. If you find any errata, please report them by visiting http://www.packtpub.com/support, selecting your book, clicking on the errata submission form link, and entering the details of your errata. Once your errata are verified, your submission will be accepted and the errata will be uploaded on our website, or added to any list of existing errata, under the Errata section of that title. Any existing errata can be viewed by selecting your title from http://www.packtpub.com/support.

Piracy

Piracy of copyright material on the Internet is an ongoing problem across all media. At Packt, we take the protection of our copyright and licenses very seriously. If you come across any illegal copies of our works, in any form, on the Internet, please provide us with the location address or website name immediately so that we can pursue a remedy.

Please contact us at `copyright@packtpub.com` with a link to the suspected pirated material.

We appreciate your help in protecting our authors, and our ability to bring you valuable content.

Questions

You can contact us at `questions@packtpub.com` if you are having a problem with any aspect of the book, and we will do our best to address it.

1
Configuration

In this chapter, we will cover the following:

- ▶ Reading the Fine Manual (RTFM)
- ▶ Planning a new database
- ▶ Changing parameters in your programs
- ▶ The current configuration settings
- ▶ Parameters that are at non-default settings
- ▶ Updating the parameter file
- ▶ Setting parameters for particular groups of users
- ▶ Basic server configuration checklist
- ▶ Adding an external module into PostgreSQL server
- ▶ Running server in power saving mode

Introduction

I get asked many questions about parameter settings in PostgreSQL.

Everybody's busy and most people want the five minute tour of how things work. That's exactly what a Cookbook does, so we'll do our best.

Some people believe that there are some magic parameter settings that will improve their performance, spending hours combing the pages of books to glean insights. Others already feel comfortable because they found some website somewhere that "explains everything", and they "know" they have their database configured OK.

For the most part, the settings are easy to understand. Finding the best setting can be difficult, and the optimal setting may change over time in some cases. This section is mostly about knowing how, when and where to change parameter settings.

Reading the Fine Manual (RTFM)

RTFM is often used rudely, meaning "don't bother me, I'm busy", or is used as a stronger form of abuse. The strange thing is that asking you to read the manual is most often very good advice. Don't flame them back, take the advice. The most important point to remember is that you should refer to a manual whose release version matches the server on which you are operating

The PostgreSQL manual is very well written, and is comprehensive in its coverage of specific topics. One of its main failings is that the "documents" aren't organized in a way that helps somebody who is trying to learn PostgreSQL. They are organized from the perspective of people checking specific technical points, so that they can decide whether their difficulty is user error or not. It sometimes answers "What?", but seldom "Why?", or 'How?"

I've helped write sections of the PostgreSQL documents as well, so I'm not embarrassed to steer you towards reading them. There are still many things to read here that are useful.

How to do it...

The main documents for each release are available at the following website:

```
http://www.postgresql.org/docs/manuals/
```

The most frequently accessed parts of the documents are as follows:

- SQL Command Reference, Client, and Server tools reference (`http://www.postgresql.org/docs/9.0/interactive/reference.html`)
- Configuration (`http://www.postgresql.org/docs/9.0/interactive/runtime-config.html`)
- Functions (`http://www.postgresql.org/docs/9.0/interactive/functions.html`)

You can also grab yourself a PDF version of the manual, which can allow easier searching in some cases. Don't print it! The documents are more than 2000 pages of A4-size sheets.

How it works...

The PostgreSQL documents are written in SGML, which is similar to, but not quite XML. These files are then processed to generate HTML or PDFs, and so on.

There's more...

There's a Wiki site on `postgresql.org` that is worth a look at as well. More information is also available at `http://wiki.postgresql.org`

Planning a new database

Planning a new database can be a daunting task. It's easy to get overwhelmed by it, so here we present some planning ideas. It's also easy to charge headlong at the task as well, thinking that the parts you know are all the things you'll ever need to consider.

Getting ready

You are ready. Don't wait to be told what to do. If you haven't been told what the requirements are, then write down what you think they are, clearly labeling them as "Assumptions" rather than "Requirements"—we mustn't confuse the two things.

Iterate until you get some agreement, and then build a prototype.

How to do it...

Write a document that covers the following items:

- **Database design**: Plan your database design.
    - Calculate the initial database sizing
- **Transaction analysis**: How will we access the database?
    - Look at the most frequent access paths
    - What are the requirements for response times?
- **Hardware configuration**
    - Initial performance thoughts—will all data fit into RAM?
- **Localization plan**
    - Decide server encoding, locale, and time zone
- **Access and security plan**
    - Identify client systems and specify required drivers
    - Create roles according to a plan for access control
    - Specify `pg_hba.conf`
- **Maintenance plan**: Who will keep it working? How?
- **Availability plan**: Consider the Availability requirements
    - `checkpoint_timeout`
    - Plan your backup mechanism and test them

▶ **High-availability plan**

     ❏   Decide what form of replication you'll need, if any

How it works...

One of the most important reasons for planning your database ahead of time is that retrofitting some things is difficult. This is especially true of server encoding and locale, which can cause much downtime and exertion if we need to change them later. Security is also much more difficult to set up after the system is live.

There's more...

Planning always helps. You may know what you're doing, but others may not. Tell everybody what you're going to do before you do it, to avoid wasting time. If you're not sure yet, then build a prototype to help decide—approach the administration framework as if it were a development task. Make a list of things you don't know yet, and work through them, one by one.

This is deliberately a very short recipe. Everybody has their own way of doing things, and it's very important not to be too prescriptive about how to do things. If you already have a plan, great. If you don't, think about what you need to do, make a checklist, and then do it.

Changing parameters in your programs

PostgreSQL allows you to set some parameter settings for each session or for each transaction.

How to do it...

You can change the value of a setting during your session, such as the following:

```
SET work_mem = '16MB';
```

This value will then be used for every future transaction. You can also change it only for the duration of the current transaction.

```
SET LOCAL work_mem = '16MB';
```

The setting will last until or if you issue the following:

```
RESET work_mem;
```
or

```
RESET ALL;
```

`SET` and `RESET` are SQL commands that can be issued from any interface. They apply only to PostgreSQL *server* parameters, by which we mean parameters that affect the server, but not necessarily the whole server. There may be other parameters, such as JDBC driver parameters, that cannot be set in this way.

How it works...

When you change the value of a setting during your session, such as:

```
SET work_mem = '16MB';
```

then this will show up in the catalog view `pg_settings` as follows:

```
postgres=# SELECT name, setting, reset_val, source
                       FROM pg_settings WHERE source = 'session';
   name   | setting | reset_val | source
----------+---------+-----------+---------
 work_mem | 16384   | 1024      | session
```

until you issue:

```
RESET work_mem;
```

after which the setting returns to the `reset_val`, and the `source` returns to default.

```
  name    | setting | reset_val | source
----------+---------+-----------+---------
 work_mem | 1024    | 1024      | default
```

There's more...

You can change the value of a setting during your transaction as well, as follows:

```
SET LOCAL work_mem = '16MB';
```

then this will show up in the catalog view `pg_settings` as follows:

```
postgres=# SELECT name, setting, reset_val
                       FROM pg_settings WHERE source = 'session';
   name   | setting | reset_val | source
----------+---------+-----------+---------
 work_mem | 1024    | 1024      | session
```

Huh? What happened to my parameter setting? SET LOCAL takes effect only for the transaction in which it was executed, which, in our case, was just the SET LOCAL command. We need to execute it inside a transaction block to be able to see the setting take hold as follows:

```
BEGIN;
SET LOCAL work_mem = '16MB';
```

then this will show up in the catalog view `pg_settings` as follows:

```
postgres=# SELECT name, setting, reset_val, source
                      FROM pg_settings WHERE source = 'session';
   name    | setting | reset_val | source
----------+---------+-----------+---------
 work_mem | 16384   | 1024      | session
```

You should also note that the value of source is "session" rather than "transaction", as you might have been expecting.

What are the current configuration settings?

At some point it will occur to you to ask, "What are the *current* configuration settings?"

How to do it...

Your first thought is probably "look in `postgresql.conf`". That works, but only as long as there is only one parameter file. If there are two, then maybe you're reading the wrong file! (How do you know?). So the cautious and accurate way is not to trust a text file, but to trust the server itself.

Also, we learned in the recipe *When to set parameters* that each parameter has a scope that determines when it can be set. Some parameters can be set through `postgresql.conf`, but others can be changed afterwards also. So the current value of configuration settings may have been subsequently changed.

We can use the `SHOW` command, such as the following:

```
postgres=# SHOW work_mem;
work_mem
----------
1MB
(1 row)
```

though remember that it reports the current setting at the time when it is run, and that can be changed in many places.

Another way of finding current settings is to access a PostgreSQL catalog view named `pg_settings`.

```
postgres=# \x
Expanded display is on.
postgres=# SELECT * FROM pg_settings WHERE name = 'work_mem';
[ RECORD 1 ] ------------
```

```
name        | work_mem
setting     | 1024
unit        | kB
category    | Resource Usage / Memory
short_desc  | Sets the maximum memory to be used for query workspaces.
extra_desc  | This much memory can be used by each internal sort
operation and hash table before switching to temporary disk files.
context     | user
vartype     | integer
source      | default
min_val     | 64
max_val     | 2147483647
enumvals    |
boot_val    | 1024
reset_val   | 1024
sourcefile  |
sourceline  |
```

So, you can use the SHOW command to retrieve the value for a setting, or you can access the full detail via the catalog table.

How it works...

Each parameter setting is cached within each session so that we have fast access to the parameter settings. That allows us to access the parameter settings with ease.

Remember that the values displayed are not necessarily settings for the server as a whole; many of those parameters will be specific to the current session. That's different than in many other databases and is also very useful.

Which parameters are at non-default settings?

Often, we need to check which parameters have been changed already or whether our changes have correctly taken effect.

How to do it...

```
postgres=# SELECT name, source, setting
                  FROM pg_settings
                  WHERE source != 'default'
                    AND source != 'override'
                  ORDER by 2, 1;
```

```
            name             |        source        |   setting
-----------------------------+----------------------+-----------
 application_name            | client               | psql
 log_timezone                | command line         | GB
 TimeZone                    | command line         | GB
 timezone_abbreviations      | command line         | Default
 archive_command             | configuration file   | (disabled)
 archive_mode                | configuration file   | off
 archive_timeout             | configuration file   | 5
 bgwriter_delay              | configuration file   | 10
 checkpoint_timeout          | configuration file   | 30
 log_checkpoints             | configuration file   | on
 log_destination             | configuration file   | stderr
 log_filename                | configuration file   | log%Y
 logging_collector           | configuration file   | on
 log_line_prefix             | configuration file   | %t[%p]
 log_min_messages            | configuration file   | log
 max_prepared_transactions   | configuration file   | 5
 max_standby_delay           | configuration file   | 90
 port                        | configuration file   | 5443
 max_stack_depth             | environment variable | 2048
 work_mem                    | session              | 204800
(29 rows)
```

How it works...

You can see from `pg_settings` which values have non-default values, and what the source of the current value is.

The `SHOW` command doesn't tell you whether a parameter is set at a non-default value. It just tells you the value, which isn't much help if you're trying to understand what is set and why.

If the source is a configuration file, then the two columns `sourcefile` and `sourceline` are also set. These can be useful in understanding where the configuration came from.

There's more...

The `setting` column of `pg_settings` shows the current value, though you can also look at `boot_val` and `reset_val`; `boot-val`, which show the value assigned when the PostgreSQL database cluster was initialized ("initdb"), while `reset_val` shows the value that the parameter will return to if you issue the `RESET` command.

Who set that?

`max_stack_depth` is an exception because `pg_settings` says it is set by the environment variable, though it is actually set by `ulimit -s` on Linux/Unix systems. `max_stack_depth` only needs to be set directly on Windows.

The timezone settings are also picked up from the OS environment, so you shouldn't need to set those directly. `pg_settings` shows this as a "command-line" setting.

Updating the parameter file

The parameter file is the main location for defining parameter values for the PostgreSQL server. All of the parameters can be set in the parameter file, which is known as the `postgresql.conf`.

There are also two other parameter files, `pg_hba.conf` and `pg_ident.conf`. Both of these relate to connections and security.

Getting ready

First, locate the `postgresql.conf` as described earlier.

How to do it...

All of the parameters can be set in the parameter file, which is known as the `postgresql.conf`. Some of the parameters take effect only when the server is first started. A typical example might be `shared_buffers`, which defines the size of the shared memory cache.

Many of the parameters can be changed while the server is still running. After changing the required parameters, we issue a `reload` operation to the server, forcing PostgreSQL to re-read the `postgresql.conf`.

```
pg_ctl -D data reload
```

The `postgresql.conf` is a normal text file that can be simply edited. Most of the parameters are listed in the file, so you can just search for them, and then overtype the desired value.

How it works...

If you set the same parameter twice in different parts of the file, the last setting is the one that applies. This can cause lots of confusion if you add settings to the bottom of the file, so you are advised against doing that.

Best practice is to either leave the file as it is and edit the values, or to start with a blank file and just include the values that you wish to change. I personally prefer a file with only the non-default values. That makes it easier to see what's happening.

Whichever method you use, you are strongly advised to keep all of the previous versions of your `.conf` files. You can do this by copying, or you can use a version control system, such as SVN.

There's more...

`postgresql.conf` also supports an include directive. This allows the postgresql.conf file to reference other files, which can then reference other files, and so on. That might help you organise your parameter settings better, if you don't make it too complicated.

Setting parameters for particular groups of users

PostgreSQL supports a variety of ways of defining parameter settings for various user groups.

How to do it...

For all users in database `saas`:

```
ALTER DATABASE saas
SET configuration_parameter = value1;
```

For a user named `simon` connected to any database, use the following:

```
ALTER ROLE simon
SET configuration_parameter = value2;
```

or set a parameter for a user only when connected to a specific database, as follows:

```
ALTER ROLE simon
IN DATABASE saas
SET configuration_parameter = value3;
```

The user won't know that these have been executed specifically for him. These are default settings, and in most cases can be overridden if the user requires non-default values.

How it works...

You can set parameters for each of the following:

- ▶ Database
- ▶ User (named "Roles" by PostgreSQL)
- ▶ Database / User combination

Each of the parameter defaults is overridden by the one below it.

In the preceding three SQL statements if:

- ▶ User hannu connects to database saas, then value1 will apply

- ▸ User simon connects to a database other than saas, then value2 will apply
- ▸ User simon connects to database saas, then value3 will apply

PostgreSQL implements this in exactly the same way as if the user had manually issued the equivalent SET statements immediately after connecting.

Basic server configuration checklist

PostgreSQL arrives configured for use on a shared system, though many people want to run dedicated database systems. The PostgreSQL project wishes to ensure that PostgreSQL will play nicely with other server software, and should not assume it has access to the full server resources. If you, as the system administrator, know that there is no other important server software running on this system, then you can crank up the values much higher.

Getting ready

Before we start, we need to know two sets of information:

First, we need to know the size of the physical RAM that will be dedicated to PostgreSQL.

Second, we need to know something about the types of applications for which PostgreSQL will be used.

How to do it...

If your database is larger than 32MB, then you'll probably benefit from increasing shared_buffers. You can increase this to much larger values, though remember that on Linux systems this memory can be swapped out if not in use, so it's better to be conservative. A new value can be set in your postgresql.conf and incremented slowly to ensure you get benefits from each change.

If you increase shared_buffers, and you're running on a non-Windows server, you will almost certainly need to increase the value of the OS parameter SHMMAX (and on some platforms others as well).

On Linux/Mac OS/FreeBSD, you will need to either edit the /etc/sysctl.conf file or use sysctl -w with the following values:

- ▸ **Linux**: kernel.shmmax=value
- ▸ **Mac OS**: kern.sysv.shmmax=value
- ▸ **FreeBSD**: kern.ipc.shmmax=value

http://www.postgresql.org/docs/8.4/static/kernel-resources.html#SYSVIPC

For example on Linux, add the following line to `/etc/sysctl.conf`:

```
kernel.shmmax=value
```

Don't worry about setting `effective_cache_size`. It is much less important a parameter than you might think; no need for too much fuss selecting the value.

If you're doing heavy write activity, then you may want to set `wal_buffers` to a much higher value than the default.

If you're doing heavy write activity and/or large data loads, you then may want to set `checkpoint_segments` higher than the default.

If your database has many large queries, you may wish to set `work_mem` to a value higher than the default.

Make sure `autovacuum` is turned on, unless you have a very good reason to turn it off. Most people don't.

To simplify some of this, I recommend that you refer to the following URL:

```
http://pgfoundry.org/projects/pgtune/
```

Leave the settings at that for now. Don't fuss too much about getting the exact settings right. You can change most of them later, so you can take an iterative approach to improving things.

Get the basics right, and keep it simple and solid. Then buy Greg Smith's book on PostgreSQL performance

Especially, don't touch `fsync` parameter. It's keeping you safe.

Adding an external module to PostgreSQL

Another one of PostgreSQL's strengths is its extensibility. Extensibility was one of the original design goals, stretching back to the late 1980s. Now, in PostgreSQL 9.0, there are many additional modules that plug into the core PostgreSQL server.

There are many kinds of additional module offerings, such as the following:

- additional functions
- additional datatypes
- additional operators
- additional indexes

Note that many tools and client interfaces work with PostgreSQL without any special installation. Here, we are discussing modules that extend and alter the behavior of the server beyond its normal range of SQL standard syntax, functions, and behaviors.

Getting ready

First, you'll need to select an appropriate module to install.

There isn't yet an automated package management system for PostgreSQL, so modules are located in a range of places, such as the following:

- Contrib— PostgreSQL "core" includes many functions. There is also an official section for add-in modules, known as "contrib" modules. These are documented at the following URL:
  - ❑ `http://www.postgresql.org/docs/9.0/static/contrib.html`

- pgFoundry— an open source development website created specifically to allow PostgreSQL modules and tools to be shared. PgFoundry uses the same software as SourceForge.net. Take a look at the following URL:
  - ❑ `http://pgFoundry.org/`

- Separate projects— large external projects, such as PostGIS, offer extensive and complex PostgreSQL modules. Take a look at the following URL:
  - ❑ `http://www.postgis.org/`

How to do it...

In some cases, modules can be added during installation if you're using a stand-alone installer application, for example, **OneClick** installer.

In other cases, you'll be able to install from a package, such as with the Oracle compatibility module `http://www.postgres.cz/index.php/Oracle_functionality`

First, we get

`http://pgfoundry.org/frs/download.php/2420/orafce-3.0.1-1.pg82.rhel5.i386.rpm`

then install using commands, such as the following:

```
rpm -ivh orafce-3.0.1-1.pg90.rhel5.i386.rpm
sudo apt-get install postgresql-8.4-orafce
```

In many cases useful modules may not have full packaging. In these cases you may need to install the module manually. This isn't very hard and is a useful exercise to help you understand what happens.

Each module will have different installation requirements. There are generally two aspects to installing a module. They are as follows:

- Installing the SQL objects for the module
- Installing the dynamic load libraries for the module

Most of the more useful modules require you to handle both of the aforementioned aspects. There are a couple of examples, such as AutoExplain, that only has dynamic load libraries.

- Build the libraries

Follow instructions for that module:

- Install the library where the server can find it:

```
shared_preload_libraries = '$libdir/modlib'
Create the database objects
psql -d dbname -f SHAREDIR/contrib/module.sql
```

How it works...

PostgreSQL can dynamically load libraries in the following three ways:

- By using the explicit LOAD command in a session
- By using `shared_preload_libraries` parameter in `postgresql.conf` at server start
- At session start, using `local_preload_libraries` parameter for a specific user, as set using ALTER ROLE

PostgreSQL functions and objects can reference code in these libraries, allowing extensions to be bound tightly into the running server process. The tight binding makes this method suitable for use even in very high-performance applications, and there's no significant difference between additional supplied features and native ones.

Running server in power saving mode

Power consumption is a hot topic. Everybody is looking for ways to do their bit for the environment. The same is true for PostgreSQL users.

Getting ready

If your PostgreSQL server is only used very sporadically, or has periods of total inactivity, then you may be able to benefit from some of the advice given here. That could be a laptop, or it could be a somewhat inactive virtual server.

How to do it...

PostgreSQL is a server-based database, so it mostly does nothing at all if there are no active clients. To minimize server activity, set the following parameters in the `postgresql.conf` file:

- `autovacuum = off`
- `wal_writer_delay = 10000`
- `bgwriter_delay = 10000`

These settings are not optimal for many uses and should only be used when it is known that the server will be quiet. They should be reset to previous values when the server becomes busy again.

How it works...

There are a couple of processes that stay active continually, on the expectation that they will be needed should clients become active. These processes are as follows:

- Writer process (also known as the "Background writer")
- WAL writer process
- Archiver, which will be active if WAL archiving is enabled
- WAL receiver process, which will be active if streaming replication is in use
- Autovacuum process

The Background writer process wakes up by default every 200ms to do its work. The maximum setting is 10s, which isn't very long, though the Background writer can be disabled by the setting, `bgwriter_lru_maxpages = 0`.

The WAL writer process wakes up by default every 200ms. The maximum setting is also 10s. This cannot be disabled. If there is no write activity, then no work will be performed, other than the wakeup and check.

The Archiver process will wake up every 15s and check whether any new WAL files have been written. This will cause some activity against the filesystem directory. That time cannot be changed by a parameter.

The WAL receiver process will wake up every 100ms to check if new replication data has arrived. If no new data has arrived, it will sleep again. That time cannot be changed by a parameter.

Autovacuum will wake up every 60s by default. This can be changed by altering the setting of `autovacuum_naptime`. Autovacuum can be disabled completely by setting `autovacuum = off`.

So, if you are using Streaming Replication, then the server will wake up every 100ms. If not, then you can reduce the wakeup time to every 10s rather than every 200ms, which is the default setting.

2
Monitoring and Diagnosis

In this chapter, we will cover the following:

- ▶ Is the user connected?
- ▶ What are they running?
- ▶ Are they active or blocked?
- ▶ Who is blocking them?
- ▶ Killing a specific session
- ▶ Resolving an in-doubt prepared transaction
- ▶ Is anybody using a specific table?
- ▶ When did anybody last use it?
- ▶ How much disk space is used by temporary data?
- ▶ Why are my queries slowing down?
- ▶ Investigating and reporting a bug
- ▶ Producing a daily summary of logfile errors

Introduction

In this chapter, you find recipes for some common monitoring and diagnosis actions you want to do inside your database. They are meant to answer specific questions that you often face when using PostgreSQL.

Monitoring is important

Databases are not isolated entities. They live on computer hardware using CPUs, RAM, and disk subsystems. Users access the database using networks. Depending on the setup, the databases themselves may need network resources to function, either by performing some authentication checks when users log in, or using disks that are mounted over the network (not generally recommended), or doing remote function calls to other databases.

This means that monitoring only the database is not enough. As a minimum, one should also monitor everything directly involved in using the database, such as the following:

- Is the database host available? Does it accept connections?
- How much of the network bandwidth is in use? Have there been network interruptions and dropped connections?
- Is there enough RAM available for most common tasks? How much is left?
- Is there enough disk space available? When will it run out of disk space?
- Is the disk subsystem keeping up? How much more load can it take?
- Can the CPU keep up with load? How much of spare idle cycles do the CPUs have?
- Are other network services the database access depends on (if any) available? For example, if you use Kerberos for authentication you have to monitor it as well.
- How many context switches are happening when the database is running?

And, for most of these things, you are interested in history, that is, how things have evolved? Was everything mostly the same yesterday? Last week? When did the disk usage start changing rapidly?

For any larger installation, you probably already have something in place for monitoring the health of your hosts and network.

The two aspects of monitoring are collecting historical data to see how things have evolved and getting alerts when things go seriously wrong. **RRDtool** (**Round Robin Database Tool**) based tools, such as **Cacti** or **Munin**, are quite popular for collecting the historical information on all aspects of the servers, and presenting this information in an easy-to-follow graphical form. Seeing several statistics on the same timescale can really help when trying to figure out why the system is behaving the way it is.

Another aspect of monitoring is getting alerts when something goes really wrong and needs (immediate) attention.

For alerting, one of the most widely-used tools is **Nagios**.

And then, of course, there is **SNMP** (**Simple Network Management Protocol)**, which is supported by a wide array of commercial monitoring solutions. Basic support for monitoring PostgreSQL through SNMP is found in `pgsnmpd`, available at the following URL:

```
http://pgsnmpd.projects.postgresql.org/
```

Providing PostgreSQL information to monitoring tools

The historical monitoring information is best to use when all of it is available from the same place and at the same timescale. Most monitoring systems have a plugin architecture, so adding new kinds of data inputs to them means installing a plugin. Sometimes, you may need to write or develop this plugin, but writing a plugin for something, such as Cacti is easy; you just have to write a script that outputs monitored values in simple text format.

Some useful things to get into graphs are number of connections, disk usage, number of queries, number of WAL files, most numbers from pg_stat_user_tables and pg_stat_user_indexes, and so on.

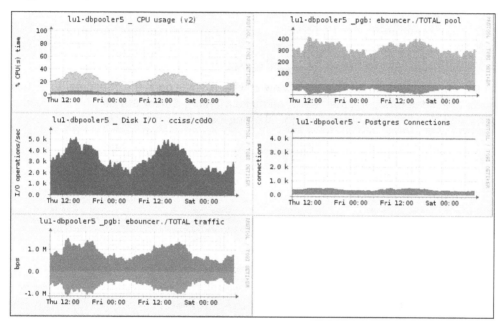

The preceding Cacti screenshot includes data for CPU, disk and network usage, pgbouncer connection pooler, and number of postgresql client connections. As you can see, they are nicely correlated.

One *Swiss Army* knife script, which can be used from both Cacti and Nagios, is check_postgres, available at http://bucardo.org/wiki/Check_postgres. It has ready-made reporting actions for a large array of things worth monitoring in PostgreSQL. Another similar effort for Nagios is available at the following URL:

http://pgfoundry.org/projects/nagiosplugins/

For Munin, there are some PostgreSQL plugins available at the Munin plugin repository at the following URL:

http://exchange.munin-monitoring.org/plugins/search?keyword=postgres

Where to find more information about generic monitoring tools

Setting up the tools themselves is a larger topic, and outside the scope of this book. In fact, each of these tools have more than one book written about them. The basic setup information and the tools themselves can be found at the following URLs:

- ▶ RRDtool (`http://www.mrtg.org/rrdtool/`)
- ▶ Cacti (`http://www.cacti.net/`)
- ▶ Munin (`http://munin-monitoring.org/`)
- ▶ Nagios (`http://www.nagios.org/`)

Realtime view using pgAdmin

You can also use pgAdmin to get a quick view of what is going on in the database. To do this, connect to the database, and then select menu item **Tools | Server Status**. This will open a window similar to the following screenshot, showing locks and running transactions:

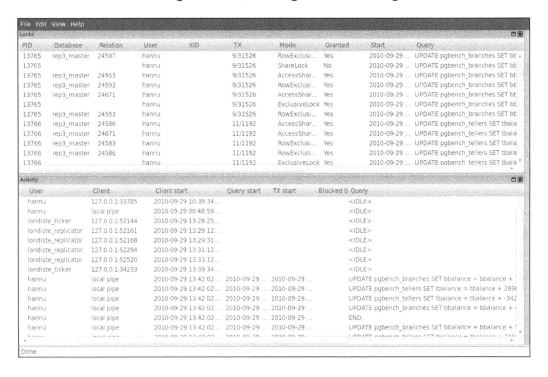

Is the user connected?

Here we show how to check if a certain database user is connected to database.

Getting ready

Make sure that you are logged in as a superuser.

How to do it...

Issue the following query to see if the user bob is connected:

```
SELECT datname FROM pg_stat_activity WHERE usename = 'bob';
```

If this query returns any rows, then database user bob is connected to database. The returned value is the name of the database to which the user is connected.

How it works...

PostgreSQL system view pg_stat_activity lists all running PostgreSQL backends, showing usernames, the SQL they are running, when they connected and when the current transaction and current query were started.

There's more...

There is more information in the pg_stat_activity view than just username.

What if I want to know "is that computer connected?"

Often, several different processes may connect as the same database user. In that case, you actually want to know if there is a connection from a specific connection.

You still can get this information from pg_stat_activity view, as it includes the connected client's IP addresses and ports. The port is only needed in case you have more than one connection from the same client computer and need to do further digging to see which process there connects to which database. Run the following:

```
SELECT datname,usename,client_addr,client_port FROM pg_stat_activity ;
```

The client_addr and client_port help you look up the exact computer, and even the process on that computer that has connected to this database.

What are they running?

Here we show how to find out which queries are currently executing

Getting ready

Make sure that you are logged in as a superuser or as the same database user you want to check.

Make sure that the parameter `track_activities` = on is set.

This can be done either in the `postgresql.conf` file or by the superuser using the following SQL statement:

```
SET track_activities = on
```

How to do it...

To see what all connected users are running now, just run the following:

```
SELECT datname,usename,current_query FROM pg_stat_activity ;
```

On systems with a lot of users, you may notice that the majority of backends are running a weird query <IDLE>. This denotes the state, where no query is actually running, and PostgreSQL is waiting for new commands from the user.

To see information for only active queries, exclude the idle ones by running the following:

```
SELECT datname,usename,current_query
FROM pg_stat_activity
WHERE current_query != '<IDLE>' ;
```

How it works...

If `track_activities` = on then PostgreSQL collects data about all running queries. Users with sufficient rights can then view this data using system view `pg_stat_activity`.

The view `pg_stat_activity` uses a system function named `pg_stat_get_activity` (procpid int) that you can use directly to watch for activity of a specific backend by supplying the process ID as an argument. Giving NULL as argument returns information for all backends.

There's more...

Sometimes you don't care about getting all queries currently running, but are just interested in seeing some of these. Or you may not like to connect to database just to see what is running.

How to catch queries which runs only for a few milliseconds

As most queries on modern **OLTP** (**Online Transaction Processing**) systems take only a few milliseconds to run, it is often hard to catch those when simply probing the `pg_stat_activity` table.

To see them actually executing you'd have to slow them down. We don't want to do that!

In PostgreSQL 9.0, there is a contrib module called pg_stat_statements that captures query execution statistics in real time. See the documentation at the following URL:

```
http://www.postgresql.org/docs/9.0/interactive/pgstatstatements.html
```

In both cases, you can script the queries and use `select pg_sleep(5)` to get the `<wait>` happen automatically. You can get subsecond waits by using floating numbers, such as `pg_sleep(0.5)` for a half second delay.

To collect the queries you just forced to be logged you can start tail `-f /var/log/postgresql/postgresql-9.0-main.log > account_queries.log` in one window, then run the preceding lock trick in another and then just use Ctrl-C to kill the tail `-f` process.

Now you have a much smaller log in account_queries.log.

How to watch longest queries

Another thing of interest for which you may want to look is long-running queries. To get a list of running queries ordered by how long they have been executing, use the following:

```
select
    current_timestamp - query_start as runtime,
    datname,
    usename,
    current_query
from pg_stat_activity
where current_query != '<IDLE>'
order by 1 desc;
```

This will return currently running queries ordered by how long they have been running, with the longest ones in front (the first field: `order by 1 desc`). On busy systems, you may want to limit the set of queries returned to only the first few ones (add `LIMIT 10` to the end), or only to queries which have been running over a certain time (for queries which have been running over one minute add `'current_timestamp – query_start 1'` min to the `WHERE` clause).

Watching queries from ps

If you want, you can also make the queries being run show up in process titles, by setting the following:

```
update_process_title = on
```

Although `ps` or `top` output is not the best place for watching the database queries; it may make sense in some circumstances.

See also

The page in PostgreSQL's online documentation, which covers related settings, is available at the following URL:

```
http://www.postgresql.org/docs/9.0/interactive/runtime-config-
statistics.html
```

Are they active or blocked?

Here we show how to find out if a query is actually running, or is it waiting for some other query.

Getting ready

Again, log in as a superuser.

How to do it...

Run the following query:

```
SELECT datname,usename,current_query
FROM pg_stat_activity
WHERE waiting = true;
```

You get a list of queries which are waiting on other backends.

How it works...

The system view `pg_stat_activity` has a boolean field `waiting`, which selects `pg_terminate_backend(procpid)` from `pg_stat_activity`, where `current_query = <IDLE>` in transaction, and `current_timestamp - query_start > '1 min'`; indicates that a certain backend is waiting on a system lock.

The preceding query uses it to filter out only queries which are waiting.

There's more...

Some more explanations about the preceding may be appropriate here.

No need for "= true"

As the column waiting is already boolean, you can safely omit the `= true` part from the query and simply write the following:

```
SELECT datname,usename,current_query
FROM pg_stat_activity
WHERE waiting;
```

This shows only queries waiting on locks

The `pg_stat_activity.waiting` field shows only if the query is waiting on a PostgreSQL internal lock.

Although this is the main cause of waiting when using pure SQL, it is possible to write something in any of the PostgreSQL's embedded languages, which can wait on other system resources, such as waiting for an http response, a file write to complete, or just waiting on timer.

An example:

Write a simple function in PL/PythonU (the **U** version means untrusted; that is, only superusers can create functions in this language):

```
create or replace function wait(seconds float)
returns void as $$
import time;
time.sleep(seconds)
$$
language plpythonu;
```

When you run the following function:

```
db=# select wait(10);
<it "stops" for 10 seconds here>
 wait
------
(1 row)
```

it will show up with as not waiting in the `pg_stat_activity` view, even though the query is in fact "blocked" on timer.

Who is blocking them?

Once you have found out that some query is blocked, you need to know who or what is blocking them.

Getting ready

Same as others, just use any superuser account to run the queries.

How to do it...

Run the following query:

```
SELECT
    w.current_query as waiting_query,
    w.procpid as w_pid,
    w.usename as w_user,
    l.current_query as locking_query,
    l.procpid as l_pid,
    l.usename as l_user,
    t.schemaname || '.' || t.relname as tablename
from pg_stat_activity w
join pg_locks l1 on w.procpid = l1.pid and not l1.granted
join pg_locks l2 on l1.relation = l2.relation and l2.granted
join pg_stat_activity l on  l2.pid = l.procpid
join pg_stat_user_tables t on l1.relation = t.relid
where w.waiting;
```

It returns process ID, user, and current query about both blocked and blocking backends, and also the schema and table name of the table that causes the blocking.

How it works...

This query first selects all waiting queries (where `w.waiting`), then gets the locks on which this query is waiting (`join pg_locks l1 on w.procpid = l1.pid` and not `l1.granted`), then looks up the lock which is granted on the same table (`join pg_locks l2 on l1.relation = l2.relation and l2.granted`), and finally looks up a row in `pg_stat_activity` corresponding to the granted lock. It also resolves the relation identifier (relid) of the table to its full name using system view `pg_stat_user_tables`.

Killing a specific session

Sometimes the only way to let the system as a whole continue is by terminating some offending database sessions.

Getting ready

Again, this is a superuser-only capability, so log in as a superuser.

How to do it...

Once you have figured out the backend you need to kill, use the function named

`pg_terminate_backend(processid)` to actually kill it.

How it works...

When a backend executes the `pg_terminate_backend(processid)` function, it sends a signal **SIGQUIT** to the backend given as an argument, after checking that the process identified by the argument `processid` actually is a PostgreSQL backend.

The backend receiving this signal stops whatever it is doing, and terminates it in a controlled way.

The client using that backend loses the connection to database. Depending on how it is written, it may silently reconnect or it may show an error to the user.

There's more...

Killing the session may not always be what you really want, so consider other options as well.

Try to cancel the query first

You may want to try a milder version `pg_cancel_backend(processid)` first.

The difference between these two is that `pg_cancel_backend()` just cancels the current query, whereas `pg_terminate_backend()` really kills the backend.

If the backend won't terminate

If `pg_terminate_backend(processid)` won't kill the backend, and you really need to reset the database state to make it continue processing requests, then you have yet another option—sending `SIGKILL` to the offending backend.

This can be done only from the command line, as root or user postgres on the same host the database is running by executing the following:

```
kill -9 <backendpid>
```

which kills that backend immediately without giving it a chance to clean up, therefore forcing the postmaster to also kill all other backends and to restart the whole cluster.

Therefore, it actually does not matter which of the PostgreSQL backends you kill.

But beware that in case you have set the parameter synchronous_commit to off, you may end up losing some supposedly *committed* transactions if you kill -9 a backend.

So kill -9 is the last resort thing to be done, only if nothing else helps, and not on a regular basis.

Use statement timeout to clean up queries which take too long

Often you know that you don't have any use for queries running more than x times. Maybe your web frontend just refuses to wait for more than 10 seconds for a query to complete and returns some default answer to users if it takes longer, abandoning the query.

In such a case, it is a good idea to set statement_timeout = 15 sec either in postgresql.conf or as a per user or per database setting, so that queries running too long don't consume precious resources and make others' queries fail as well.

The queries terminated by statement timeout show up in log as follows:

```
hannu=# set statement_timeout = '3 s';
SET
hannu=# select wait(10);
ERROR:  canceling statement due to statement timeout
```

They used to show up as a more confusing "query canceled due to user request" on the older version of PostgreSQL.

Killing "Idle in transaction" queries

Sometimes, people start a transaction, run some queries, and then just leave without ending the transaction. This can leave some system resources in a state where some housekeeping processes can't be run or they may even have done something more serious, such as locking a table, thereby causing immediate *denial of service* for other users needing that table.

You can use the following query to kill all backends that have an open transaction but have been doing nothing for the last 10 minutes:

```
select pg_terminate_backend(procpid)
  from pg_stat_activity
where current_query = '<IDLE> in transaction'
   and current_timestamp - query_start > '10 min';
```

You can even schedule this to be running every minute while you are trying to find the specific PHP frontend, which keeps leaving open transactions behind, or you have a lazy administration leaving psql connection open, or a flaky network that drops clients without the server noticing it.

You can also kill the backend from command line

Another possibility to terminate a backend is by using a Unix/Linux command named `kill N`, which sends the signal to process `N` on the system where it is running. You have to be either the root user or the user running the database backends (usually postgres) to be able to send signals to processes.

Resolving an in-doubt prepared transaction

When using 2PC (two phase commit), you may end up in a situation where you have locked something, but cannot find a backend that holds the locks.

For example:

```
db=# select t.schemaname || '.' || t.relname as tablename,
db-# l.pid, l.granted
db-# from pg_locks l join pg_stat_user_tables t
db-# on l.relation = t.relid;
 tablename |  pid  | granted
-----------+-------+---------
    db.x   |       | t
    db.x   | 27289 | f
(2 rows)
```

has a lock on table `db.x`, which has no process associated with it. If you see this then check pg_prepared_xacts to see if there are any in-doubt prepared transactions that ness resolving.

Is anybody using a specific table?

This one helps you when you are in doubt if some obscure table is used any more, or is it just leftover from old times that just takes up space.

Getting ready

Make sure that you are a superuser, or at least have full rights on the table in question.

How to do it...

To see if a table is currently in active use, that is, if anyone is using it while you watch, run the following:

```
create temp table tmp_stat_user_tables as select * from pg_stat_user_
tables;
```

Then wait a little, and see what is changed.

```
select * from pg_stat_user_tables n
  join tmp_stat_user_tables t
    on n.relid=t.relid
    and (n.seq_scan,n.idx_scan,n.n_tup_ins,n.n_tup_upd,n.n_tup_del) <>
(t.seq_scan,t.idx_scan,t.n_tup_ins,t.n_tup_upd,t.n_tup_del);
```

How it works...

The table `pg_stat_user_tables` is a view that shows current statistics for table usage.

To see if a table is used, you check for changes in its usage counts.

The previous query selects all tables where any of the usage counts for selector data manipulation have changed.

There's more...

The quick and dirty way

If you are sure that you have no use for the cumulative statistics gathered by PostgreSQL, you can just reset all table statistics by doing

```
select pg_stat_reset()
```

This sets all statistics to 0, and you can detect table use by just looking for tables where any usage count is not 0

Of course, you can make a backup copy of statistics table first, as follows:

```
create table backup_stat_user_tables as
select current_timestamp as snaptime, *
from  pg_stat_user_tables;
```

Collecting daily usage statistics

It is often useful to have historical usage statistics of tables available when trying to solve performance problems or just understanding the usage patterns.

For this purpose, you can collect the usage data in a regular manner daily or even more often using either cron or a PostgreSQL-specific scheduler like `pg_agent`.

The following query adds a timestamped snapshot of current usage statistics to the table created earlier:

```
insert into backup_stat_user_tables
select current_timestamp as snaptime, *
from   pg_stat_user_tables;
```

When did anybody last use it?

Once you find out that a table is not used currently, the next question is "when was it last used?"

Getting ready

Get access to the database as a superuser or to the database host computer as user postgres.

How to do it...

PostgreSQL does not have any built-in last-used information about tables, so you have to use other means to figure it out.

If you have set up a cronjob to collect usage statistics, as described in the previous section, then it is relatively easy to find out the last change date using an SQL query.

Else, you have basically two possibilities, neither of which gives you absolutely reliable answers.

You can either look at actual timestamps of the files in which the data is stored, or you can use the `xmin` and `xmax` system columns to find out the latest transaction ID that has changed the table data.

Looking at file dates

To find out the file name(s) in which the table data is stored, you have to do the following:

Here is a sample PL/PythonU function that lists main file statistics for files used to store a table. You need to have PL/PythonU installed in your database for this to work. If you don't have it, use the following:

```
CREATE LANGUAGE plpythonu;
```

to install the language in the database. This assumes you have the support for PL/PythonU available on the database host.

First, we create a return type for the function, and then the function itself as follows:

```
CREATE TYPE fileinfo AS (
  filename text,
  filesize bigint,
  ctime abstime,
  mtime abstime,
  atime abstime
  );
CREATE OR REPLACE FUNCTION table_file_info(schemaname text, tablename
text)
RETURNS SETOF fileinfo
AS $$
import datetime, glob, os
db_info = plpy.execute("""
select datname as database_name,
       current_setting('data_directory') || '/base/' || db.oid as
data_directory
  from pg_database db
 where datname = current_database()
""")
#return db_info[0]['data_directory']
table_info_plan = plpy.prepare("""
select nspname as schemaname,
       relname as tablename,
       relfilenode as filename
  from pg_class c
  join pg_namespace ns on c.relnamespace=ns.oid
 where nspname = $1
   and relname = $2;
""", ['text', 'text'])
table_info = plpy.execute(table_info_plan, [schemaname, tablename])
filemask = '%s/%s*' % (db_info[0]['data_directory'], table_info[0]
['filename'])
res = []
for filename in glob.glob(filemask):
    fstat = os.stat(filename)
    res.append((
      filename,
      fstat.st_size,
      datetime.datetime.fromtimestamp(fstat.st_ctime).isoformat(),
      datetime.datetime.fromtimestamp(fstat.st_mtime).isoformat(),
      datetime.datetime.fromtimestamp(fstat.st_atime).isoformat()
    ))
return res
$$ LANGUAGE plpythonu;
```

Now, you can see the latest modification and access times for a table using the following query:

```
select
    max(mtime) as latest_mod,
    max(atime) as latest_read
from table_file_info(<schemaname>, <tablename>);
```

How it works...

The function `table_file_info(schemaname, tablename)` returns creation, modification, and access times for files used by PostgreSQL to store the table data.

The last query uses this data to get the latest time any of these files were modified or read by PostgreSQL. This is not a very reliable way to get information about the latest *use* of any table, but it gives you a rough upper-limit estimate about when it was last modified or read.

If you have shell access to the database host, then you can carry out the preceding steps by hand, say in case you can't or don't want to install PL/PythonU for some reason.

You can also get the information using built-in functions `pg_ls_dir(dirname text)` and `pg_stat_file(filename text)`. For example, the following query:

```
select pg_ls_dir, (select modification from pg_stat_file(pg_ls_dir))
as modtime from pg_ls_dir('.');
```

lists all files and directories in PostgreSQL data directory.

There's more...

There may be last-use information in future version of PostgreSQL

There has been some discussion recently about adding last-used data to the information PostgreSQL keeps about tables, so it is entirely possible that answering the question "When did anybody last use this table?" will be much easier in the next version of PostgreSQL.

How much disk space is used by temporary data?

In addition to ordinary stable tables, you can also create temporary tables.

Also, PostgreSQL may use temporary files for query processing if it can't fit all the needed data to memory.

So, how do you find out how much data is used by temporary tables and files?

Getting ready

Same as previous—you can do this using any untrusted embedded language, or directly on the database host. You have to use an untrusted language, because trusted ones run in a sandbox, which prohibits them from accessing the host file system directly.

How to do it...

First, check if your database defines special tablespaces for temporary files as follows:

```
select current_setting('temp_tablespaces');
```

When temp_tablespaces has one or more tablespaces

If it does, then your task is easy, because all temporary files, both for temporary table and those used for query processing, are inside the directories for these tablespaces—just look up the corresponding directories from `pg_tablespaces` as follows:

```
select spcname,spclocation from pg_tablespace;
```

Then, a simple `du` command shows you the space used by temporary files.

A sample session is as follows:

```
db=# select current_setting('temp_tablespaces');
 current_setting
-----------------
 temp1, temp2
(1 row)
db=#
db=# select spcname,spclocation from pg_tablespace where spcname in
('temp1', 'temp2');
 spcname |   spclocation
---------+----------------
 temp1   | /test/pg_tmp1
 temp2   | /test/pg_tmp2
(2 rows)
db=# \q
user@host:~$
sudo du -s /test/pg_tmp1 /test/pg_tmp2
102136 /test/pg_tmp1
35144  /test/pg_tmp2
```

Because the amount of temporary disk space used can vary a lot on an active system, you may want to repeat the last `du -s` command several times to get a better picture of how the disk usage changes.

When temp_tablespaces is empty

If the `temp_tablespaces` setting is empty, then the temporary tables are stored in the same directory as ordinary tables, and temp files used for query processing are stored in the `pgsql_tmp` directory inside the main database directory.

Look up the clusters home directory as follows:

```
select current_setting('data_directory') || '/base/pgsql_tmp'
```

The size of this directory gives the total size of current temporary files for query processing.

The total size of temporary files used by this database can be found by running the following query:

```
select sum(pg_total_relation_size(relid))
   from pg_stat_all_tables
where schemaname like 'pg_%temp%';
```

How it works...

Because all the temporary tables and other temporary on-disk data are stored in files, you use PostgreSQL's internal tables to find the location of these files, and then determine the total size of these files.

There's more...

While the preceding information about temporary tables is correct, it is not the wholes story.

Finding out if temporary file is in use any more

Because temporary files are not carefully preserved as ordinary tables (this is actually one of the benefits of temporary tables, as less bookkeeping makes them faster) it may sometimes happen that a system crash can leave around some temporary files, which can, in worst cases, take up a significant amount of disk space.

As a rule, you can clean up such files by shutting down the PostgreSQL server, and then deleting all files from the `pgsql_temp` directory.

Logging temporary file usage

If you set `log_temp_files = 0` or a larger value, then the creation of all temporary files that are larger than this value in kilobytes are logged to standard PostgreSQL log.

Why are my queries slowing down?

Queries that used to run in tens of milliseconds suddenly take several seconds.

A summary query for a report that used to run in a few seconds takes half an hour to complete.

Here are some ways to find out what is slowing them down.

Getting ready

Any questions of type "why is this different today than it was last week?", are much easier to answer if you have some kind of historic data collecting set up.

Things such as Cacti or Munin for monitoring general server characteristics (CPU and RAM usage, disk I/O, network traffic, load average) are very useful to see what has changed recently, and to try to correlate this with observed performance of some database operations.

Also, collecting historic statistics data from `pg_stat_*` tables, be that daily, hourly, or even every five minutes if you have enough disk space, is also very useful for detecting possible causes for sudden changes or gradual degradation in performance.

If you have both these statistics gatherings going on, then even better. If you have none, then the question is actually "Why is this query slow?".

But don't despair, because there are some things you can do to try to restore performance.

How to do it...

First, analyze your database as follows:

```
db_01=# analyse;
ANALYZE
Time: 6231.313 ms
db_01=#
```

This is the first thing to try, as it is usually cheap and is meant to be run quite often anyway.

If this restores the query performance, or at least improves current performance considerably, then it means that `autovacuum` is not doing its job well, and the next thing to do is to check why it is so.

How it works...

ANALYZE updates statistics about data size and data distribution in all tables. If a table size has changed significantly without its statistics being updated, then PostgreSQL's statistics-based optimizer can choose a bad plan. Running the ANALYZE command manually, updates the statistics for all tables.

There's more...

There are a few other common problems.

Do the queries return significantly more data than earlier?

If you initially tested your queries on almost empty tables, it is entirely possible that you are querying much more data than you need.

As an example, if you select all users items, and then show the first 10, then this runs very fast when user has 10 or even 50 items, but not so well when he/she has 50,000 rows.

Check that you don't ask for more data than you need; use the LIMIT clause to return less data to your application This will give the optimizer a chance to select a plan which processes less data when selecting and may also have lower startup cost.

Do the queries also run slowly when run alone?

If you can, then try to run the same slow query when the database has no or very little other queries running concurrently.

If it runs well in this situation, then it may be that the database host is just overloaded (CPU, memory, or disk I/O) and a plan that worked well under light load, is not so good any more. It may even be that it is not a very good query plan with which to begin, and you were fooled by modern computers being really fast.

```
db=# select count(*) from t;
  count
---------
 1000000
(1 row)
Time: 329.743 ms
```

As you can see, scanning one million rows takes just 0.3 seconds on a laptop, a few years old, if these rows are already cached.

But, if you have a few of such queries running in parallel, and also other queries competing for memory, this query can slow down an order of magnitude or two.

Is the second run of same query also slow?

This test is related to the previous one, and it checks if the slowdown may be caused by some of the needed data not fitting in memory, or being pushed out of memory by other queries.

If the second run of the query is fast, then you probably have developed a problem of not enough memory.

See also

▶ *Is anybody using a specific table/Collecting daily usage* statistics shows one way to collect info on table changes

Investigating and reporting a bug

When you find out that PostgreSQL is not doing what it should, then it's time to investigate.

Getting ready

It is a good idea to make a full copy of your PostgreSQL installation before you start investigating. This will help you restart several times and be sure that you are in fact investigating the results of the bug and not chasing your own tail by looking at changes introduced by your last investigation and debugging attempt.

How to do it...

Try to make a minimal repeatable test scenario which exhibits this bug. Sometimes the bug disappears while doing it, but mostly it is needed for making it easier for the one who tries to fix it. It is almost impossible to fix a bug that you can't observe and repeat at will.

If it is about query processing, then usually you can provide minimal dump file (result of running `pg_dump`) of your database together with an SQL script that exhibits the error.

If you have corrupt data, then you may want to make (a subset of) the corrupted data files available to people who have knowledge and time to look at it. Sometimes, you can find such people on the PostgreSQL hackers list, and sometimes you have to hire someone or even fix it yourself. The more preparatory work you do yourself and the better you formulate your questions, the higher is the chance you have of finding help quickly.

If you suspect a data corruption bug and feel adventurous, then you can read about the data formats at `http://www.postgresql.org/docs/9.0/static/storage.html`, and investigate your data tables using the `pageinspect` package from contrib.

And always include at least the PostgreSQL version you are using and the operating system on which you are using it.

For a full guide, see the end of this chapter.

How it works...

If everything works really well, then it goes like the following:

- ▶ A user submits a well-researched bug report to the PostgreSQL bugs list
- ▶ Some discussions follow on the list and the user may be asked to provide some additional information
- ▶ Somebody finds out what is wrong, and proposes a fix
- ▶ The fix is discussed on the hackers list
- ▶ The bug is fixed, there is a patch for current version and, the fix will be included in the next version
- ▶ Sometimes the fix is backported to older versions

Unfortunately, this can go wrong at each step, due to various reasons, such as nobody feeling that this is his/her area of expertise, the right people not having time and hoping for someone else to deal with it, and these other people may just not be reading the list at the right moment.

If this happens, follow up your question in a day or two to try to understand why there was no reaction.

See also

The official PostgreSQL bug/problem reporting guides

If you follow the following URLs, you have a high chance of getting your questions answered:

`http://wiki.postgresql.org/wiki/Guide_to_reporting_problems`

`http://wiki.postgresql.org/wiki/SlowQueryQuestions`

Producing a daily summary of logfile errors

PostgreSQL can generate gigabytes of logs per day. Lots of data is good in case you want to investigate some specific event, but it is not what you will use for daily monitoring of database health.

Getting ready

Make sure that your PostgreSQL is set up to rotate the log files daily.

A default setup will do exactly the following:

```
log_rotation_age = 1d
```

Then get a PostgreSQL log processing program. Here, we describe how to do it using **pgFouine**.

For most Linux systems, you should be able to use your default package manager to install pgFouine.

Configure your PostgreSQL to produce `logfiles` in a format that pgFouine understands. Select logging to `syslog`. Use a modern version of `syslogd` for high-traffic databases.

How to do it...

Set up a cron job to run a few minutes after the default log rotation time. You can find the time by looking at timestamps of already rotated log files; they all have similar times.

Run the following:

```
pgfouine.php -file /var/log/postgressql/postgresql-9.0-main.log.1
-reports n-mostfrequenterrors > errors.html
```

You can also set it up to e-mail the generated error report to the DBA at that time.

How it works...

PgFouine condenses and ranks error messages for easy viewing, and produces a nicely formatted report in HTML. From that report, you can find out the most frequent errors.

As a rule, it is a good practice not to tolerate errors in database logs if you can avoid it. Once the errors start showing up in the log and report, you should find the cause of the errors and fix them.

While it is tempting to leave the errors there, as *they do no harm* and consider them just a small nuisance, it is often true, that simple errors are indication of other problems in the application, which if not found and understood may lead to all kinds of larger problems, such as security breaches or eventual data corruption at the logical level.

There's more...

Writing your own log processor

If you have only a small number of errors in your log files, then it may be sufficient to just run each logfile through `grep` to find errors:

```
user@dbhost: $ egrep "FATAL|ERROR" postgresql-9.0-main.log
```

See also

► Home page for pgFouine is at the following website:

  `http://pgfouine.projects.postgresql.org/`

► You can get much more information on setting up pgFouine at the following URL:

  `http://pgfouine.projects.postgresql.org/tutorial.html`

► Another similar tool is **PQA (Practical Query Analysis)**, available at the following URL:

  `http://pqa.projects.postgresql.org/`

PQA is written in **Ruby**, so if you are good at using Ruby, you may prefer this one .

In PostgreSQL 9.0, there is also a contrib module `pg_stat_statements` that captures query execution statistics in real time. See the documentation at the following URL:

`http://www.postgresql.org/docs/9.0/interactive/pgstatstatements.html`

3
Regular Maintenance

In this chapter, we will cover the following:

- ▶ Controlling automatic database maintenance
- ▶ Avoiding auto freezing and page corruptions
- ▶ Avoiding transaction wraparound
- ▶ Removing old prepared transactions
- ▶ Actions for heavy users of temporary tables
- ▶ Identifying and fixing bloated tables and indexes
- ▶ Maintaining indexes
- ▶ Finding unused indexes
- ▶ Carefully removing unwanted indexes
- ▶ Planning maintenance

Introduction

PostgreSQL prefers regular maintenance, and there is a recipe discussing planning maintenance.

We recognize that you're here for a reason and are looking for a quick solution to your needs. You're probably thinking fix me first and I'll plan later. So off we go.

PostgreSQL provides a utility command named VACUUM, which is a jokey name for a garbage collector that sweeps up all the bad things and fixes them, or at least most of them. That's the single most important thing you need to remember to do—I say single thing because closely connected to that is the ANALYZE command, that collects optimizer statistics. It's possible to run VACUUM and ANALYZE as a single joint command VACUUM ANALYZE, plus those actions are automatically executed for you when appropriate by autovacuum, a special background process that forms part of the PostgreSQL server.

VACUUM performs a range of clean up activities, some of them too complex to describe without a whole sideline into internals. VACUUM has been heavily optimized over a 10-year period to take the minimum required lock levels on tables, and execute in the most efficient manner possible, skipping all unnecessary work, and using L2 cache CPU optimizations when work is required.

Many experienced PostgreSQL DBAs will prefer to execute their own VACUUMs, though autovacuum now provides a fine degree of control, and that can save you much time by enabling and controlling it. Using both manual and automatic vacuuming gives you both control and a safety net.

Controlling automatic database maintenance

Autovacuum is enabled by default in PostgreSQL 9.0, and mostly does a great job of maintaining your PostgreSQL database. I say mostly because it doesn't know everything you do about the database, such as when would be the best time to perform maintenance actions.

Getting ready

Exercising control requires some thinking about what you actually want:

- Which are the best times of day to do things? When are system resources more available?
- Which days are quiet, and are which not?
- Which tables are critical to the application, and which are not?

How to do it...

The first thing to do is to make sure autovacuum is switched on. You must have both the following parameters enabled in your `postgresql.conf`:

- `autovacuum = on`
- `track_counts = on`

PostgreSQL controls autovacuum with 35 individually tunable parameters. That provides a wide range of options, though can be a little daunting.

The following parameters can be set in `postgresql.conf`:

- `autovacuum`
- `autovacuum_analyze_scale_factor`
- `autovacuum_analyze_threshold`

- `autovacuum_freeze_max_age`
- `autovacuum_max_workers`
- `autovacuum_naptime`
- `autovacuum_vacuum_cost_delay`
- `autovacuum_vacuum_cost_limit`
- `autovacuum_vacuum_scale_factor`
- `autovacuum_vacuum_threshold`
- `log_autovacuum_min_duration`

Individual tables can be controlled by "storage parameters", which are set using the following:

```
ALTER TABLE mytable SET (storage_parameter = value);
```

The storage parameters that relate to maintenance are as follows:

- `autovacuum_enabled`
- `autovacuum_vacuum_cost_delay`
- `autovacuum_vacuum_cost_limit`
- `autovacuum_vacuum_scale_factor`
- `autovacuum_vacuum_threshold`
- `autovacuum_freeze_min_age`
- `autovacuum_freeze_max_age`
- `autovacuum_freeze_table_age`
- `autovacuum_analyze_scale_factor`
- `autovacuum_analyze_threshold`

and "toast" tables can be controlled with the following parameters:

- `toast.autovacuum_enabled`
- `toast.autovacuum_vacuum_cost_delay`
- `toast.autovacuum_vacuum_cost_limit`
- `toast.autovacuum_vacuum_scale_factor`
- `toast.autovacuum_vacuum_threshold`
- `toast.autovacuum_freeze_min_age`
- `toast.autovacuum_freeze_max_age`
- `toast.autovacuum_freeze_table_age`
- `toast.autovacuum_analyze_scale_factor`
- `toast.autovacuum_analyze_threshold`

How it works...

If autovacuum is set, then autovacuum will wake up every autovacuum_naptime seconds, and decide whether to run VACUUM and/or ANALYZE commands.

There will never be more than autovacuum_max_workers maintenance processes running at any one time. As these autovacuum slaves perform I/O, they accumulate cost points, until they hit the autovacuum_vacuum_cost_limit, after which they sleep for autovacuum_vacuum_cost_delay. This is designed to throttle the resource utilization of autovacuum to prevent it from using all available disk performance, which it should never do. So, increasing autovacuum_vacuum_cost_delay will slow down each VACUUM to reduce the impact on user activity. Autovacuum will run an ANALYZE command when there have been at least autovacuum_analyze_threshold changes, and a fraction of the table defined by autovacuum_analyze_scale_factor has been inserted, updated, or deleted.

Autovacuum will run a VACUUM command when there have been at least autovacuum_vacuum_threshold changes, and a fraction of the table defined by autovacuum_vacuum_scale_factor has been updated or deleted.

If you set log_autovacuum_min_duration, then any autovacuum that runs for longer than this value will be logged to the server log, like the following:

```
2010-04-29 01:33:55 BST (13130) LOG:  automatic vacuum of table
"postgres.public.pgbench_accounts": index scans: 1
    pages: 0 removed, 3279 remain
    tuples: 100000 removed, 100000 remain
    system usage: CPU 0.19s/0.36u sec elapsed 19.01 sec
2010-04-29 01:33:59 BST (13130) LOG:  automatic analyze of table
"postgres.public.pgbench_accounts"
    system usage: CPU 0.06s/0.18u sec elapsed 3.66 sec
```

Most of the preceding global parameters can also be set at the table level. For example, if you think that you don't want a table to be autovacuumed, then you can set:

```
ALTER TABLE big_table SET (autovacuum_enabled = off);
```

It's also possible to set parameters for **toast** tables. The toast table is the location where oversize column values get placed, which the documents refer to as "supplementary storage tables". If there are no oversize values, then the toast table will occupy little space. Tables with very wide values often have large toast tables. TOAST (stands for **the oversize attribute storage technique**) is optimized for UPDATE. If you have a heavily updated table, the toast table is untouched, so it may makes sense to turn off autovacuuming of the toast table as follows:

```
ALTER TABLE pgbench_accounts
SET ( autovacuum_vacuum_cost_delay = 20
        ,toast.autovacuum_enabled = off);
```

which will turn off autovacuuming of the "toast" table.

Note that autovacuuming of the toast table is performed completely separately from the main table, even though you can't ask for an explicit include/exclude of the toast table yourself when running VACUUM.

Use the following query to display the reloptions for tables and their toast tables:

```
postgres=# SELECT n.nspname, c.relname,
                  pg_catalog.array_to_string(c.reloptions || array(
                    select 'toast.' ||
                    x from pg_catalog.unnest(tc.reloptions) x),', ')
                  as relopts
FROM pg_catalog.pg_class c
  LEFT JOIN
          pg_catalog.pg_class tc ON (c.reltoastrelid = tc.oid) JOIN
          pg_namespace n ON c.relnamespace = n.oid
WHERE c.relkind = 'r'
AND nspname NOT IN ('pg_catalog', 'information_schema');
  nspname |       relname        |         relopts
---------+-------------------+-----------------------------
  public | pgbench_accounts  | fillfactor=100,

                                autovacuum_enabled=on,

                                autovacuum_vacuum_cost_delay=20
  public | pgbench_tellers   | fillfactor=100
  public | pgbench_branches  | fillfactor=100
  public | pgbench_history   |
  public | text_archive      | toast.autovacuum_enabled=off
```

VACUUM allows inserts, updates, and deletes while it runs, though it prevents actions such as ALTER TABLE and CREATE INDEX. Autovacuum can detect if a user requests a conflicting lock on the table while it runs, and will cancel itself if it is getting in the user's way.

Note that VACUUM does not shrink a table when it runs, unless there is a large run of space at the end of a table, and nobody is accessing the table when we try to shrink it. To properly shrink a table, you need VACUUM FULL. That locks up the whole table for a long time, and should be avoided, if possible. VACUUM FULL will literally rewrite every row of the table, and completely rebuild all indexes. That process is faster in 9.0 than it used to be, though it's still a long time for larger tables.

There's more...

`postgresql.conf` also allows "include directives", which look like the following:

```
include 'autovacuum.conf'
```

These specify another file that will be read at that point, just as if those parameters had been included in the main file.

This can be used to maintain multiple sets of files for autovacuum configuration. Let's say we have a website that is busy, mainly during the daytime, with some occasional night time use. We decide to have two profiles, one for daytime, when we want only less aggressive autovacuuming, and another at night, where we allow more aggressive vacuuming.

We add the following lines to `postgresql.conf`:

- `autovacuum = on`
- `autovacuum_max_workers = 3`
- `include 'autovacuum.conf'`

and remove all other autovacuum parameters.

We then create one file named `autovacuum.conf.day`, containing the following parameters:

- `autovacuum_analyze_scale_factor = 0.1`
- `autovacuum_analyze_threshold = 50`
- `autovacuum_vacuum_cost_delay = 30`
- `autovacuum_vacuum_cost_limit = -1`
- `autovacuum_vacuum_scale_factor = 0.2`
- `autovacuum_vacuum_threshold = 50`

and another file named `autovacuum.conf.night`, that contains the following parameters:

- `autovacuum_analyze_scale_factor = 0.05`
- `autovacuum_analyze_threshold = 50`
- `autovacuum_vacuum_cost_delay = 10`
- `autovacuum_vacuum_cost_limit = -1`
- `autovacuum_vacuum_scale_factor = 0.1`
- `autovacuum_vacuum_threshold = 50`

To swap profiles, we would simply do the following actions:

```
$ ln -sf autovacuum.conf.night autovacuum.conf
$ pg_ctl -D datadir reload          # server reload command
```

(customized depending upon your platform).

This then allows us to switch profiles twice per day without needing to edit the configuration files. You can also tell easily which is the active profile simply by looking at the full details of the linked file (using ls –l). The exact details of the schedule are up to you; night/day was just an example, which is unlikely to suit everybody.

See also

`autovacuum_freeze_max_age` is explained in the recipe *Avoiding auto freezing*, as are the more complex table-level parameters.

Avoiding auto freezing and page corruptions

There are some aspects of VACUUM that are complex to explain why they exist, though have some occasional negative behaviors. Let's look more deeply at those and find some solutions.

Getting ready

PostgreSQL performs regular sweeps to clean out old transaction identifiers, which is known as "freezing". It does this to defer transaction wraparound, which is discussed in more detail in the next recipe.

There are two routes that a row can take in PostgreSQL: the row version dies and needs to be removed by VACUUM, or a row version gets old enough to need to be frozen, also performed by the VACUUM process.

Why do we care? Say we load a table with 100 million rows. Everything is fine. When those rows have been there long enough to begin being frozen, the next VACUUM on that table will re-write all of these rows to freeze their transaction identifiers. Put that another way, autovacuum will wake up and start using lots of I/O to perform the freezing.

How to do it...

The most obvious way to forestall that exact problem is to explicitly VACUUM a table after a major load. Of course that doesn't remove the problem entirely, and you might not have time for that.

Many people's knee-jerk reaction is to turn off autovacuum, because it keeps waking up at the most inconvenient times. My way is described in the recipe, *Controlling automatic database maintenance*.

Freezing takes place when a transaction identifier on a row becomes more than vacuum_ freeze_min_age transactions older than the current next value. Normal VACUUMs will perform a small amount of freezing as you go, and in most cases, you won't notice at all. As explained in the earlier example, large transactions leave many rows with the same transaction identifiers, so those might cause problems at freezing time.

VACUUM is normally optimized to look only at chunks of a table that require cleaning. When a table reaches vacuum_freeze_table_age, we ignore that optimization, and scan the whole table. While it does so, it's fairly likely to see rows that need freezing, which need to be re-written. So that is what causes the great increase in I/O.

If you fiddle with those parameters to try to forestall heavy VACUUMs, then you'll find that the `autovacuum_freeze_max_age` parameter controls when the table will be scanned by a forced VACUUM. To put that another way, you can't turn off the need to freeze rows, but you can get to choose when this happens. My advice is to control autovacuum as described in previous recipe, or perform explicit VACUUMs at a time of your choosing.

VACUUM is also an efficient way to confirm the absence of page corruptions, so it is worth scanning the whole database from time-to-time, every block. To do this, you can run the following script on each of your databases:

```
SET vacuum_freeze_table_age = 0;
VACUUM;
```

You can do this table-by-table as well; there's nothing special about whole database VACUUMs anymore—in earlier versions of PostgreSQL this was important, so you may read in random places on the web that this is a good idea.

If you've never had a corrupt block, then you may only need to scan maybe every two-to-three months. If you start to get corrupt blocks, then you may want to increase the scan rate to confirm everything is OK. Corrupt blocks are usually hardware-induced, though they show up as database errors. It's possible but rare that the corruption was instead from a PostgreSQL bug.

There's no easy way to fix page corruptions at present. There are ways to investigate and extract data from corrupt blocks, for example, using the contrib/pageinspect utility I wrote.

Avoiding transaction wraparound

To many users, "transaction wraparound" sounds like a disease from space. Mentioning "transaction wraparound" usually earns the speaker points for technical merit. Let's take a look at it, and how to avoid it.

Getting ready

First: have you seen the following message?

WARNING: database "postgres" must be vacuumed within XXX transactions.

HINT: To avoid a database shutdown, execute a database-wide VACUUM in that database.

You might also need to commit or roll back old prepared transactions.

Or even worse, the following message:

ERROR: database is not accepting commands to avoid wraparound data loss in database "template0"

HINT: Stop the postmaster and use a standalone backend to vacuum that database.

You might also need to commit or roll back old prepared transactions.

If not, then you don't need to do anything apart from normal planned maintenance. Those messages are reported to users, and they are also written to the server log.

How to do it...

If you have a support provider, now is a good time to call. Don't panic, but technical bravado can land you in worse situations than in which you already are. Let's continue to describe how to get out of this.

If you've received the WARNING, then follow both hints. First, let's do the suggested VACUUM on the appropriate database; it might not be "postgres", so replace the appropriate database name.

Either run the following:

```
$ vacuumdb postgres
```

or use the following:

```
psql -c "VACUUM" postgres
```

or use your admin tool to initiate a VACUUM on the appropriate database.

Next, find and follow the recipe, *Removing old prepared transactions*.

How it works...

PostgreSQL uses internal transaction identifiers that are four bytes long, so we only have 2^31 transaction ids (about two billion). PostgreSQL wraps around and starts again from the beginning when that wraps around, allocating new identifiers in a circular manner. The reason we do this is that moving to an eight-byte identifier has various other negative effects and costs that we would rather not pay, so we keep the four-byte transaction identifier, which also has costs.

PostgreSQL is designed to continue using ids even after the system wraps. Properly maintained, everything will keep working forever and you'll never notice what happens on the inside. To allow that to happen we need to run regular VACUUMs.

There's more...

If you received the aforementioned ERROR, and the database is no longer accepting commands you're probably wondering what the phrase use a standalone backend to vacuum that database means.

A "standalone backend" means running the database server from just a single executable process. This is the equivalent of *nix run-level 1, also known as single user mode. We restrict access to the database to just a single user.

The command to do this is the following, noting that the --single must be the very first command on the command line:

```
$ postgres --single -D  /full/path/to/datadir postgres
```

which then returns the following command line prompt:

```
PostgreSQL stand-alone backend 9.0

backend>
```

and you can then run the VACUUM from there, as follows:

```
PostgreSQL stand-alone backend 9.0

backend> VACUUM;

backend>
```

when you're finished, type <CTRL>-D (or whatever you have set EOF to be for your terminal window) once or twice if you also used the -j option.

You should also check for old prepared transactions as described in *Removing old prepared transactions*.

The recipe, *Avoiding auto freezing*, may also be relevant, or at least be an interesting read in a related area.

Removing old prepared transactions

You may have been routed here from other recipes, so you might not even know what prepared transactions are, let alone what an old one looks like.

The good news is that prepared transactions don't just happen, they happen in certain specific situations. If you don't know what I'm talking about, it's OK, you won't need to, and better still, you probably don't have any either.

Prepared transactions are part of the "two-phase commit" feature, also known as **2PC**. A transaction commits in two stages rather than one, allowing multiple databases to have synchronized commits. It's typical use is to combine multiple "resource managers" using the XA protocol, usually provided by a **Transaction Manager** (**TM**), as used by the **Java Transaction API** (**JTA**) and others. If none of that meant anything to you, then you probably don't have any prepared transactions.

Getting ready

First, check the setting of max_prepared_transactions. If this is zero, then you don't have any. If you still have no idea what I'm talking about, then set the parameter to zero.

```
SHOW max_prepared_transactions;
```

If your setting is more than zero, then look to see if you have any. As an example, you may find something like the following:

```
postgres=# SELECT * FROM pg_prepared_xacts;
-[ RECORD 1 ]------------------------------
transaction | 121083
gid         | prep1
prepared    | 2010-03-28 15:47:57.637868+01
owner       | postgres
database    | postgres
```

where the gid ("global identifier") will usually have been automatically generated.

How to do it...

Removing a prepared transaction is also referred to as "resolving in-doubt transactions". The transaction is literally stuck between committing and aborting. The database or transaction manager crashed, leaving the transaction mid-way through the two-phase commit process.

If you have a connection pool of 100 active connections and something crashes, you'll probably find 1 to 20 transactions stuck in the prepared state, depending upon how long your average transaction is.

To resolve the transaction, we need to decide whether we want that change, or not. The best way is to check what happened externally to PostgreSQL. That should help you decide.

If you do need further help, look at the *There's more* section.

If you wish to commit the changes, then:

```
COMMIT PREPARED 'prep1';
```

or if you want to rollback the changes then:

```
ROLLBACK PREPARED 'prep1';
```

How it works...

Prepared transactions are persistent across crashes, so you can't just do a fast restart to get rid of them. They have both an internal transaction identifier and an external "global identifier". Either of those can be used to locate locked resources, and decide how to resolve the transactions.

There's more...

If you're not sure what the prepared transaction actually did, you can go and look, though it is time consuming. The pg_locks view shows locks are held by prepared transactions. You can get a full report of what is being locked using the following query:

```
postgres=# SELECT l.locktype, x.database, l.relation, l.page,
                  l.tuple,l.classid, l.objid, l.objsubid,
                  l.mode, x.transaction, x.gid, x.prepared,
                  x.owner
           FROM pg_locks l JOIN pg_prepared_xacts x
           ON l.virtualtransaction = '-1/' ||
                  x.transaction::text;
```

The documents mention that you can join `pg_locks` to `pg_prepared_xacts`, though they don't mention that if you join directly on the transaction id, all it tells you is that there is a transaction lock, unless there are some row-level locks. The table locks are listed as being held by a virtual transaction. A simpler query is the following:

```
postgres=# SELECT DISTINCT x.database, l.relation
           FROM pg_locks l JOIN pg_prepared_xacts x
           ON l.virtualtransaction = '-1/' ||
              x.transaction::text
           WHERE l.locktype != 'transactionid';
 database  | relation
-----------+----------
 postgres  |    16390
 postgres  |    16401
(2 rows)
```

This tells you which relations in which databases have been touched by the remaining prepared transactions. We can't tell the names because we'd need to connect to those databases to check.

You can then fully scan each of those tables, looking for changes like the following:

```
SELECT * FROM table WHERE xmin = 121083;
```

which will show you all the rows in that table inserted by transaction `121083`, taken from the transaction column of `pg_prepared_xacts`.

Actions for heavy users of temporary tables

If you are a heavy user of temporary tables in your applications, then there are some additional actions you may need to perform.

How to do it...

There are four main things to check, which are as follows:

1. Make sure you run VACUUM on system tables, or enable autovacuum to do this for you.
2. Monitor running queries to see how many and how large temporary files are active.
3. Tune memory parameters. Think about increasing the temp_buffers parameter, though be careful not to overallocate memory by doing so.
4. Separate temp table I/O. In a query intensive system, you may find that read/write to temporary files exceeds reads/writes on permanent data tables and indexes. In this case, you should create new tablespace(s) on separate disks, and ensure that the `temp_tablespaces` parameter is configured to use the additional tablespace(s).

How it works...

In PostgreSQL 9.0, when we create a temporary table, we insert entries into the catalog tables pg_class and pg_attribute. These catalog tables and their indexes begin to grow and to bloat, an issue covered in later recipes. To control that growth, you can either VACUUM those tables manually, or set autovacuum = on in postgreql.conf. You cannot run ALTER TABLE against system tables, so it is not possible to set specific autovacuum settings for any of these tables.

If you VACUUM the system catalog tables manually, make sure you get all of the system tables. You can get the full list of tables to VACUUM using the following query:

```
postgres=# SELECT relname, pg_relation_size(oid)
            FROM pg_class
            WHERE relkind in ('i','r') and relnamespace = 11
            ORDER BY 2 DESC;
```

relname	pg_relation_size
pg_proc	450560
pg_depend	344064
pg_attribute	286720
pg_depend_depender_index	204800
pg_depend_reference_index	204800
pg_proc_proname_args_nsp_index	180224
pg_description	172032
pg_attribute_relid_attnam_index	114688
pg_operator	106496
pg_statistic	106496
pg_description_o_c_o_index	98304
pg_attribute_relid_attnum_index	81920
pg_proc_oid_index	73728
pg_rewrite	73728
pg_class	57344
pg_type	57344
pg_class_relname_nsp_index	40960

... (partial listing)

The preceding values are for a newly created database. These tables can get very large if not properly maintained, with values of 11 GB of for one index being witnessed at one unlucky installation.

Identifying and fixing bloated tables and indexes

PostgreSQL implements **MVCC (Multi-Version Concurrency Control)**, that allows users to read data at the same time as writers make changes. This is an important feature for concurrency in database applications, as it can allow the following:

- Better performance because of fewer locks
- Greatly reduced deadlocking
- Simplified application design and management

MVCC is a core part of PostgreSQL and cannot be turned off, nor would you really want it to be. The internals of MVCC have some implications for the DBA that need to be understood. The price for these benefits is that SQL UPDATE command can cause tables and indexes to grow in size because they leave behind dead row versions. DELETEs and aborted INSERTs take up space that must be reclaimed by garbage collection. **VACUUM** is the mechanism by which we reclaim space, though there is also another internals feature named **HOT**, which does much of this work automatically for us.

Knowing this, many people become worried by and spend much time trying to rid themselves of dead row versions. Many users will be familiar with tools to perform tasks, such as defragmentation, shrinking, reorganization, and table optimization. These things are necessary, though you should not be unduly worried by the need for vacuuming in PostgreSQL. Many users execute VACUUM far too frequently, while at the same time complaining about the cost of doing so.

This recipe is all about understanding when you need to run VACUUM by estimating the amount of bloat in tables and indexes.

How to do it...

The best way to understand things is to look at things the same way that autovacuum does. Use the following query, derived by Greg Smith for his *PostgreSQL 9.0 High Performance* book, also by *Packt*. The calculations are derived directly from the autovacuum documentation.

```
CREATE OR REPLACE VIEW av_needed AS
SELECT *,
  n_dead_tup > av_threshold AS "av_needed",
  CASE WHEN reltuples > 0
    THEN round(100.0 * n_dead_tup / (reltuples))
    ELSE 0
    END AS pct_dead
FROM
(SELECT
```

```
  N.nspname, C.relname,
  pg_stat_get_tuples_inserted(C.oid) AS n_tup_ins,
  pg_stat_get_tuples_updated(C.oid) AS n_tup_upd,
  pg_stat_get_tuples_deleted(C.oid) AS n_tup_del,
  pg_stat_get_tuples_hot_updated(C.oid)::real /
  pg_stat_get_tuples_updated(C.oid) AS HOT_update_ratio,
  pg_stat_get_live_tuples(C.oid) AS n_live_tup,
  pg_stat_get_dead_tuples(C.oid) AS n_dead_tup,
  C.reltuples AS reltuples,round(
     current_setting('autovacuum_vacuum_threshold')::integer
    +current_setting('autovacuum_vacuum_scale_factor')::numeric
* C.reltuples)
    AS av_threshold,  date_trunc('minute',greatest(pg_stat_get_last_
vacuum_time(C.oid),pg_stat_get_last_autovacuum_time(C.oid))) AS last_
vacuum, date_trunc('minute',greatest(pg_stat_get_last_analyze_time(C.
oid),pg_stat_get_last_analyze_time(C.oid))) AS last_analyze
 FROM pg_class C LEFT JOIN
  pg_index I ON C.oid = I.indrelid
  LEFT JOIN pg_namespace N ON (N.oid = C.relnamespace)
  WHERE C.relkind IN ('r', 't')
    AND N.nspname NOT IN ('pg_catalog', 'information_schema') AND
    N.nspname !~ '^pg_toast'
) AS av
ORDER BY av_needed DESC,n_dead_tup DESC;
```

which we can then use to look at individual tables as follows:

```
postgres=# \x
postgres=# SELECT * FROM av_needed
                WHERE relation = 'public.pgbench_accounts';
-[ RECORD 1 ]----+-------------------------
nspname          | public
relname          | pgbench_accounts
n_tup_ins        | 100001
n_tup_upd        | 117201
n_tup_del        | 1
hot_update_ratio | 0.123454578032611
n_live_tup       | 100000
n_dead_tup       | 0
reltuples        | 100000
av_threshold     | 20050
last_vacuum      | 2010-04-29 01:33:00+01
last_analyze     | 2010-04-28 15:21:00+01
av_needed        | f
pct_dead         | 0
```

How it works...

We can compare the number of dead row versions, shown as `n_dead_tup` against the required threshold, `av_threshold`.

The above query doesn't take into account table-specific autovacuum thresholds. It could do if you really need that, though the main purpose of the query is to give us information to understand what is happening, and then set the parameters accordingly, not the other way around.

Notice that the table query shows insert, updates and deletes, so you can understand your workload better. There is also something named the `HOT_update_ratio`. This shows the fraction of updates that take advantage of the HOT feature, which allows a table to self-vacuum as the table changes. If that ratio is high, then you may avoid VACUUMs altogether, or at least for long periods. If the ratio is low, then you will need to execute VACUUMs or autovacuums more frequently. Note that the ratio never reaches 1.0, so if you have better than 0.95, then that is very good, and you need not think about it further.

HOT updates take place when the UPDATE statement does not change any of the column values that are indexed by any index. If you change even one column that is indexed by just one index then it will be a non-HOT update, and there will be a performance hit. So careful selection of indexes can improve update performance and reduce the need for maintenance. Also, if HOT updates do occur, though not often enough for your liking, you might try to decrease the fillfactor storage parameter for the table. Remember that this will only be important on your most active tables. Seldom-touched tables don't need much tuning.

So, to recap: non-HOT updates cause indexes to bloat. The following query is useful in investigating index size, and how that changes over time. It runs fairly quickly, and can be used to monitor whether your indexes are changing in size over time.

```
SELECT
    nspname,relname,
    round(100 * pg_relation_size(indexrelid) /
                pg_relation_size(indrelid)) / 100
        AS index_ratio,
    pg_size_pretty(pg_relation_size(indexrelid))
        AS index_size,
    pg_size_pretty(pg_relation_size(indrelid))
        AS table_size
FROM pg_index I
LEFT JOIN pg_class C ON (C.oid = I.indexrelid)
LEFT JOIN pg_namespace N ON (N.oid = C.relnamespace)
WHERE
  nspname NOT IN ('pg_catalog', 'information_schema', 'pg_toast') AND
  C.relkind='i' AND
  pg_relation_size(indrelid) > 0;
```

Another route is to use the contrib/pgstattuple module, supplied with PostgreSQL. This provides overkill statistics about what's happening in your tables and indexes, which it derives by scanning the whole table or index, and literally counting everything. It's very good, and I am not dismissing it. Just use carefully: if you have time to scan the table, you may as well have VACUUMed the whole table anyway.

Scan tables using `pgstattuple()` as follows:

```
test=> SELECT * FROM pgstattuple('pg_catalog.pg_proc');
-[ RECORD 1 ]------+-------
table_len          | 458752
tuple_count        | 1470
tuple_len          | 438896
tuple_percent      | 95.67
dead_tuple_count   | 11
dead_tuple_len     | 3157
dead_tuple_percent | 0.69
free_space         | 8932
free_percent       | 1.95
```

and scan indexes using `pgstatindex()` as follows:

```
postgres=> SELECT * FROM pgstatindex('pg_cast_oid_index');
-[ RECORD 1 ]------+-------
version            | 2
tree_level         | 0
index_size         | 8192
root_block_no      | 1
internal_pages     | 0
leaf_pages         | 1
empty_pages        | 0
deleted_pages      | 0
avg_leaf_density   | 50.27
leaf_fragmentation | 0
```

There's more...

You may want this as a Nagios plugin.

Look at **check_postgres_bloat** as part of the **check_postgres** plugins. That provides some flexible options to assess bloat. Unfortunately, its not that well documented, though if you've read this, it should make sense. You'll need to play with it to get the thresholding correct anyway, so that shouldn't be a problem.

Note also that the only way to know for certain the exact bloat of a table or index is to scan the whole relation. Anything else is just an estimate, and might lead to you running maintenance either too early or too late.

Maintaining indexes

Indexes can become a problem in many database applications that involve a high proportion of inserts/deletes. Just as tables can become bloated, so do indexes.

In the last recipe we saw that non-HOT updates can cause bloated indexes. Non-primary key indexes are also prone to some bloat from normal inserts, as is common in most relational databases.

Autovacuum does not detect bloated indexes, nor does it do anything to rebuild indexes. So we need to look at ways to maintain indexes.

Getting ready

PostgreSQL supports commands that will rebuild indexes for you. The client utility **reindexdb** allows you to execute the REINDEX command in a convenient way from the operating system:

```
$ reindexdb
```

This executes the SQL REINDEX command on every table in the default database. If you want to reindex all databases, then use the following:

```
$ reindexdb -a
```

That's what the manual says anyway. My experience is that most indexes don't need rebuilding, and even if they do, REINDEX puts a full table lock (AccessExclusiveLock) on the table while it runs. That locks up your database for possibly hours, and I advise that you think about *not* doing that.

Try this recipe *instead*.

First, let's create a test table with two indexes: a primary key and an additional index as follows:

```
DROP TABLE IF EXISTS test;
CREATE TABLE test
(id INTEGER PRIMARY KEY
,category TEXT
, value TEXT);
CREATE INDEX ON test (category);
```

Now, let's look at the internal identifier of the tables, the `oid`, and the current file number, or `relfilenodes` as shown next:

```
SELECT oid, relname, relfilenode
FROM pg_class
WHERE oid in (SELECT indexrelid
                FROM pg_index
                WHERE indrelid = 'test'::regclass);
  oid  |       relname        | relfilenode
-------+----------------------+-------------
 16639 | test_pkey            |       16639
 16641 | test_category_idx    |       16641
(2 rows)
```

How to do it...

PostgreSQL supports a command known as CREATE INDEX CONCURRENTLY, that builds an index without taking a full table lock. PostgreSQL also supports the ability to have two indexes, with different names, that have exactly the same definition. So, the trick is to build another index identical to the one you wish to rebuild, drop the old index, and then rename the new index to the same name as the old index had. Et voila, fresh index, no locking. Let's see that in slow motion:

```
CREATE INDEX CONCURRENTLY new_index
ON test (category);
BEGIN;
DROP INDEX test_category_idx;
ALTER INDEX new_index RENAME TO test_category_idx;
COMMIT;
```

and if we check our internal identifiers again, we get the following:

```
SELECT oid, relname, relfilenode
FROM pg_class
WHERE oid in (SELECT indexrelid
                FROM pg_index
                WHERE indrelid = 'test'::regclass);
  oid  |       relname        | relfilenode
-------+----------------------+-------------
 16639 | test_pkey            |       16639
 16642 | test_category_idx    |       16642
(2 rows)
```

So, we can see that `test_category_idx` is now a completely new index.

That seems pretty good, yet it doesn't work on primary keys. Why not? Because you can't add a primary index to a table concurrently, in PostgreSQL 9.0 at least.

So we have another trick, slightly more complex than the last. First, we create another index with the same definition as the primary key as follows:

▶   `CREATE UNIQUE INDEX new_pkey ON test (id);`

and check internal identifiers again as follows:

```
SELECT oid, relname, relfilenode
FROM pg_class
WHERE oid in (SELECT indexrelid
              FROM pg_index
              WHERE indrelid = 'test'::regclass);
  oid  |      relname       | relfilenode
-------+--------------------+-------------
 16639 | test_pkey          |       16639
 16642 | test_category_idx  |       16642
 16643 | new_pkey           |       16643
(3 rows)
```

Now we're going to swap the two indexes over, so that all the primary key constraints stay active and so do all of the foreign keys that depend upon them. So, we need to swap the `relfilenode` values as follws:

```
BEGIN;
LOCK TABLE test;
UPDATE pg_class SET relfilenode = 16643 WHERE oid = 16639;
UPDATE pg_class SET relfilenode = 16639 WHERE oid = 16643;
DROP INDEX new_pkey;
COMMIT;
```

which we confirm has succeeded using the following:

```
SELECT oid, relname, relfilenode
FROM pg_class
WHERE oid in (SELECT indexrelid
              FROM pg_index
              WHERE indrelid = 'test'::regclass);
  oid  |      relname       | relfilenode
-------+--------------------+-------------
 16639 | test_pkey          |       16643
 16642 | test_category_idx  |       16642
 16643 | new_pkey           |       16639
(3 rows)
```

Yes, that's right. We just updated the core internal catalog tables of PostgreSQL. So make a mistake here, and you're in a big world of hurt. Make sure your backups are nicely polished before doing this.

How it works...

CREATE INDEX CONCURRENTLY allows inserts, updates, and deletes while the index is being created. It cannot be executed inside another transaction, and only one per table can be created at any time.

Swapping the indexes is easy and doesn't use any trickery.

Swapping the primary keys used some internals knowledge. The indexes themselves don't know which numbers they are, so you can swap them over without problems—as long as you swap the correct two indexes, and they really do have identical definitions. Be especially careful about creating the indexes in the same tablespace, as the above will fail if they're different.

There's more...

If you are fairly new to database systems, you might think rebuilding indexes for performance is something that only PostgreSQL needs to do. Other DBMS require this also, just maybe don't say so.

Indexes are designed for performance, and in all databases, deleting index entries causes contention and loss of performance. PostgreSQL does not remove index entries for a row when that row is deleted, so an index can fill with dead entries. PostgreSQL does attempt to remove dead entries when a block becomes full, though that doesn't stop small numbers of dead entries accumulating in many data blocks.

See also

I'm writing this just as PostgreSQL 9.0 is coming out. Its likely that in later versions, we will get a simple REINDEX CONCURRENTLY command that can be used more easily.

Locating the unused indexes

Selecting the correct set of indexes for a workload is known to be a hard problem. It usually involves trial and error by developers and DBAs to get a good mix of indexes.

Tools exist to identify slow queries and many SELECT statements can be improved by the addition of an index.

What many people forget is to check whether the mix of indexes remains valuable over time, which is something for the DBA to investigate and optimize.

How to do it...

PostgreSQL keeps track of each access against an index. We can view that information and use it to see if an index is unused as follows:

```
postgres=# SELECT schemaname, relname, indexrelname, idx_scan FROM pg_
stat_user_indexes ORDER BY idx_scan;
 schemaname  |         indexrelname       | idx_scan
-------------+----------------------------+----------
 public      | pgbench_accounts_bid_idx   |        0
 public      | pgbench_branches_pkey      |    14575
 public      | pgbench_tellers_pkey       |    15350
 public      | pgbench_accounts_pkey      |   114400
(4 rows)
```

As we can see in the preceding code, there is one index that is totally unused, alongside others that have some usage. You now need to decide whether "unused" means you should remove the index. That is a more complex question, and we first need to explain how it works.

How it works...

The PostgreSQL statistics accumulate various useful information. These statistics can be reset to zero using an administrator function. Also, as the data accumulates over time, we usually find that objects that have been there longer have higher apparent usage. So if we see a low number for `idx_scan`, then it might be that the index was newly created (as was the case in my preceding demonstration), or it might be that the index is only used by a part of the application that runs only at certain times of day, week, month, and so on.

Another important consideration is that the index may be a unique constraint index that exists specifically to safeguard against duplicate inserts. An INSERT does *not* show up as an `idx_scan`, whereas an UPDATE or DELETE might, because they have to locate the row first. So, a table that only has INSERTs against it will appear to have unused indexes.

Also, some indexes that show usage might be showing usage that was historical, and there is no further usage. Or, it might be the case that some queries use an index where they could just as easily and almost as cheaply use an alternative index. Those things are for you to explore and understand before you take action.

See also

You may decide from this that you want to remove an index. If only there was a way to try removing an index and then put it back again quickly if you cause problems! Rebuilding an index might take hours on a big table, so these decisions can be a little scary. No worries, just follow the next recipe, *Carefully removing unwanted indexes*.

Carefully removing unwanted indexes

Carefully removing? You mean press "enter" gently after typing DROP INDEX? err, no.

The thinking is that it takes a long time to build an index, and a short time to drop one. What we want is a way of removing the index that if we discover that removing it was a mistake, we can put the index back again quickly.

How to do it...

First, create the following function:

```
CREATE OR REPLACE FUNCTION trial_drop_index(iname TEXT)
RETURNS VOID
LANGUAGE SQL AS $$
UPDATE pg_index
SET indisvalid = false
WHERE indexrelid = $1::regclass;
$$;
```

then, run it to do a trial of dropping the index.

If you experience performance issues after dropping the index, then use the following function to "undrop" the index:

```
CREATE OR REPLACE FUNCTION trial_undrop_index(iname TEXT)
RETURNS VOID
LANGUAGE SQL AS $$
UPDATE pg_index
SET indisvalid = true
WHERE indexrelid = $1::regclass;
$$;
```

How it works...

This recipe also uses some inside knowledge. When we create an index using CREATE INDEX CONCURRENTLY, it is a two-stage process. The first phase builds the index, and then marks it invalid. Inserts, updates, and deletes now begin maintaining the index, but we do a further pass over the table to see if we missed anything before we declare the index valid. User queries don't use the index until it says valid.

Once the index is built and the flag is valid, then if we set the flag to invalid, the index will still be maintained, just not used by queries. This allows us to turn the index off quickly, though with the option to turn it back on again if we realize we actually do need the index after all. This makes it practical to test whether dropping the index will alter the performance of any of your most important queries.

Planning maintenance

In these busy times many people believe "if it ain't broke, don't fix it". I believe that also, though it isn't an excuse for not taking action to maintain your database servers and be sure that nothing will break.

Database maintenance is about making your database run smoothly.

Monitoring systems are not a substitute for good planning. They alert you to unplanned situations that need attention. The more unplanned things you respond to, the greater the chance that you will need to respond to multiple emergencies at once. And when that happens, something will break. Ultimately that is your fault. If you wish to take your responsibilities seriously you should plan ahead.

How to do it...

- **Let's break a rule**: If you don't have a backup, take one *now*. I mean now, go on, off you go. Then let's talk some more about planning maintenance. If you already do, well done. It's hard to keep your job as a DBA if you lose data because of missing backups, especially today when everybody's grandmother knows to keep her photos backed up.

- **First, plan your time**: Make a regular date on which to perform certain actions. Don't allow yourself to be a puppet of your monitoring system, running up and down every time the lights change. If you keep being dragged off on other assignments then you'll need to make it clear that you need to get a good handle on the database maintenance to make sure it doesn't bite you.

- **Don't be scared**: It's easy to worry about what you don't know and either overreact or underreact to the situation. Your database probably doesn't need to be inspected daily, but never is definitely a bad place also.

How it works...

Build a regular cycle of activity around the following tasks:

- **Capacity planning**: Observing long term trends in system performance and keeping track of growth of database volumes. Plan in to the schedule any new data feeds, new projects that increase rates of change. Best done monthly, so you monitor what has happened and what will happen.

- **Backups, recovery testing, and emergency planning**: Organize regular reviews of written plans, test scripts, check tape rotation, confirm that you still have the password to the off-site backups, and so on. Some sysadmins run a test recovery every night so they always know that a successful recovery is possible.

- **Vacuum and index maintenance**: To reduce bloat, including collecting optimizer statistics through ANALYZE.

- Consider VACUUM again, with the need to manage the less frequent **freezing** process. This is listed as a separate task so that you don't ignore this and have it bite you later.

- **Server log file analysis**: How many times has the server restarted? Are you sure you know about each incident?

- **Security and intrusion detection**: Has your database already been hacked? What did they do?

- **Understanding usage patterns**: If you don't know much about what your database is used for then I'll wager it is not very well tuned or maintained.

- **Long term performance analysis**: It's a common occurrence for me to get asked to come and tune a system which is slow. Often what happens is that a database server can get slower over a very long period. Nobody ever noticed any particular day when it got slow, it just got slower over time. Keeping records of response times over time can help confirm whether or not everything is as good now as it was months or years previously. This activity is where you might reconsider current index choices.

Many of these activities are mentioned in this chapter or throughout the rest of the cookbook. Some are not because they aren't so much technical tasks but more just planning and understanding of your environment.

You might also find time to consider the following things:

- **Data quality:** Are the contents of the database accurate and meaningful? Could the data be enhanced?

- **Business intelligence**: Is the data being used for everything that can bring value to the organization?

Index

about 8
reference link 8
working 8
PQA (Practical Query Analysis) 47

Q

queries
blocking, causes 32
long-running queries, viewing 29
slowing down, causes 42, 44
status, verifying 30
viewing, from ps 30
queries, running for milliseconds
catching 29

R

regular maintenance
about 50
actions, for heavy users of temporary
tables 61, 62
auto freeze, avoiding 55, 56
automatic database maintenance,
controlling 50, 51
bloated tables and indexes, fixing 63
bloated tables and indexes, identifying 63
indexes, maintaining 67-70
maintenance, planning 73
old prepared transactions, removing 59
page corruptions, avoiding 55, 56
transaction wraparound, avoiding 56, 57
unwanted indexes, removing 72
REINDEX CONCURRENTLY command 70
RRDtool (Round Robin Database Tool)
about 24
Cacti 24
Munin 24
RTFM 8
Ruby 47

S

Separate projects 19
SET LOCAL command 11
SHOW command 12
SIGQUIT signal 33

**SNMP (Simple Network Management Proto-
col) 24**
SQL REINDEX command 67
storage parameters
autovacuum_analyze_scale_factor 51
autovacuum_analyze_threshold 51
autovacuum_enabled 51
autovacuum_freeze_max_age 51
autovacuum_freeze_min_age 51
autovacuum_freeze_table_age 51
autovacuum_vacuum_cost_delay 51
autovacuum_vacuum_cost_limit 51
autovacuum_vacuum_scale_factor 51
autovacuum_vacuum_threshold 51
Swiss knife script 25

T

table
daily usage statistics, collecting 36
file dates, viewing 37, 39
status, verifying 35
temporary data
space consumption, measuring 39
temp_tablespaces settings 40, 41
temporary file usage
logging 41
temp_tablespaces parameter 61
transaction wraparound
avoiding 56, 57

U

unwanted indexes
removing 72

V

VACUUM command 49

W

WAL receiver process 22
WAL writer process 21

Thank you for buying
PostgreSQL 9 Administration Cookbook: LITE

About Packt Publishing

Packt, pronounced 'packed', published its first book "*Mastering phpMyAdmin for Effective MySQL Management*" in April 2004 and subsequently continued to specialize in publishing highly focused books on specific technologies and solutions.

Our books and publications share the experiences of your fellow IT professionals in adapting and customizing today's systems, applications, and frameworks. Our solution based books give you the knowledge and power to customize the software and technologies you're using to get the job done. Packt books are more specific and less general than the IT books you have seen in the past. Our unique business model allows us to bring you more focused information, giving you more of what you need to know, and less of what you don't.

Packt is a modern, yet unique publishing company, which focuses on producing quality, cutting-edge books for communities of developers, administrators, and newbies alike. For more information, please visit our website: www.packtpub.com.

About Packt Open Source

In 2010, Packt launched two new brands, Packt Open Source and Packt Enterprise, in order to continue its focus on specialization. This book is part of the Packt Open Source brand, home to books published on software built around Open Source licences, and offering information to anybody from advanced developers to budding web designers. The Open Source brand also runs Packt's Open Source Royalty Scheme, by which Packt gives a royalty to each Open Source project about whose software a book is sold.

Writing for Packt

We welcome all inquiries from people who are interested in authoring. Book proposals should be sent to author@packtpub.com. If your book idea is still at an early stage and you would like to discuss it first before writing a formal book proposal, contact us; one of our commissioning editors will get in touch with you.

We're not just looking for published authors; if you have strong technical skills but no writing experience, our experienced editors can help you develop a writing career, or simply get some additional reward for your expertise.

LITE Code: S5MU7ZM1RBH9

www.ingramcontent.com/pod-product-compliance
Lightning Source LLC
Chambersburg PA
CBHW060456060326
40689CB00020B/4548